W9-BHE-385

The Nuclear Years

"AND What's New With You?"

—from *Herblock's Here and Now* (Simon & Schuster, 1955)

THE
NUCLEAR
YEARS

The Arms Race and Arms Control, 1945-70

Chalmers M. Roberts

PRAEGER PUBLISHERS
New York • Washington • London

PRAEGER PUBLISHERS

111 Fourth Avenue, New York, N.Y. 10003, U.S.A.
5, Cromwell Place, London S.W.7, England

Published in the United States of America in 1970
by Praeger Publishers, Inc.

© 1970 by Praeger Publishers, Inc.

Library of Congress Catalog Card Number: 70–112978

Printed in the United States of America

For Lois, who has shared the nuclear years with me, and for David, Patricia, and Christopher, in the hope that, through wisdom born of knowledge, their generation and succeeding generations may escape a nuclear holocaust.

Contents

Preface

"We must have some international sanity to cope with this thing."

I find that sentence in a letter I wrote to my wife on November 7, 1945, just after having visited Hiroshima. Ten days and twenty-four years later, I watched in the Yellow Room of the Finnish Government's banquet hall Smolna, in Helsinki, as representatives of the United States and the Soviet Union gathered to open the Washington-Moscow strategic arms limitation talks, which have come to be known as the SALT talks, despite the redundancy. I cite these matters to give the reader what he is entitled to: some reason to feel that the author of this book has, at the least, a considerable acquaintance with the events that have shaped the nuclear years.

As to almost all other Americans, the Bomb was a total surprise to me when President Truman revealed to the world its development and its first use on August 6, 1945. As a junior officer in the U.S. Army Air Corps (now the Air Force) working in the Pentagon in Far East Intelligence, I had been privy to many military and diplomatic secrets. But of the Bomb I knew nothing. Soon after the end of World War II, I went to Japan (where I had lived and worked in 1938 and 1939) as a member of the U.S. Strategic Bombing Survey to interrogate Japanese officers and officials. On October 27, I visited Nagasaki, where the second bomb had been exploded on August 9, and on November 7, I visited Hiroshima.

Reading now the letters I wrote home about those two experiences, some three months after the Bomb had been used the first two times (the only times, thus far, in war), I vividly recall the horror of it.

First impressions generally lack scientific accuracy, but they can sear the mind. "The people who were there may have been vaporized for thousands were instantly killed," I wrote. "The blast effect was terrific. [Hiroshima] is far worse than Nagasaki because it is flat and the blast traveled further before it ran into mountains. . . . The appearance of devastation is terrific, trees are stripped, poles are down and rubble, rubble, rubble is everywhere. . . . Most of the city's doctors were killed the first day. . . . They say that people protected against the rays by three feet of concrete were not affected by direct radiation, though possibly by indirect radiation. Burns killed the bulk of those who died, of whom there is no firm or accurate figure."

The Hiroshima and Nagasaki bombs were, by today's standards, relative miniatures, dropped from aircraft. Each of them packed about 20 kilotons of explosive force, the equivalent of 20,000 tons of TNT. Since the advent of the H-bomb, nuclear weapons have made the quantum jump to megatons. Rival American and Soviet intercontinental missiles today carry from 1 to 25 megatons in their single warheads. The largest single nuclear explosion to date was that of a 1961 test in the Soviet Union, a blast of 60 megatons —the equivalent of 60 million tons of TNT—3,000 times the force of the bombs used against Japan.

Like most Americans in 1945, I accepted the use of the Bomb against Japan as a means of saving American lives that we thought would otherwise have been lost in an invasion. And, too, like most of those in the armed services, I doffed uniform as quickly as possible to return to peaceful pursuits.

Not until 1953 did I have reason to begin to grapple with the problems the Bomb had posed. That year I began to write about nuclear weapons when I first was assigned by the *Washington Post* to be its diplomatic reporter. My job has since led me to numerous international conferences, including all the Soviet-American summit meetings of national leaders, at which nuclear weapons more and more were at issue.

This book grew from an effort to summarize for the *Washington Post*, on the eve of the SALT talks, the history of the nuclear years, both the arms race and the efforts to control or curb it. The book is meant to be a short history for those who wish to re-explore the past quarter-century, or who are too young to remember it.

Naturally, I owe much to others: first, to the editors of the *Washington Post*, who have given me the opportunity to follow this fascinating, though so often disheartening, and increasingly complex story for so many years; second, to my colleagues at the *Washington Post*, Murrey Marder, now the newspaper's diplomatic reporter, and Howard Simons, long the paper's science reporter and now assistant managing editor, both of whom have shared many of the stories of these years with me, and to Herbert Block, whose pen (over the signature of Herblock) has so well illuminated the problems of the age; also, to many in the U.S. Government and in other governments who have been so helpful to me in the past seventeen years; and, finally, to the many others who have written in this field.

Washington, D.C.
March, 1970

The Nuclear Years

From Hiroshima to the SALT Talks

Bernard M. Baruch, a veteran of the disastrous Versailles Peace Conference after World War I, pulled his chair up to the table, adjusted his pince-nez, and began to read:

> We are come to make a choice between the quick and the dead. That is our business. Behind the black portent of the new atomic age lies a hope which, seized upon with faith, can work our salvation. If we fail, then we have damned every man to be the slave of Fear. Let us not deceive ourselves: We must elect World Peace or World Destruction.

The day was June 14, 1946. The place, the newborn United Nations' temporary headquarters at New York's Hunter College in the Bronx. Baruch was President Harry S. Truman's representative at the U.N. Atomic Energy Commission.

The tone of Baruch's speech had been determined a few days earlier. In his accustomed way, he had sat on a park bench in New York with two friends, discussing the remarks he was soon to make. He said he wanted to convey that the question the delegates were about to consider was a matter of life and death for the world. Later, as he was to recount in *My Own Story,** one of his

---

* Publication data on this and all books mentioned hereafter can be found in the Bibliography.

park-bench companions, Herbert Bayard Swope, phoned to say, "I've got your opening line. It comes from the best possible source —the Bible."

Thus began the quest for man's control of the cataclysmic power he had unleashed when he learned to split the atom.

What follows is a review of the efforts, now in their twenty-fifth year, to control some or all aspects of nuclear weapons with the hope of curbing their growth in power and their proliferation in numbers and types—or even, in some Utopian future, of eliminating them.

The post-World War II history of nuclear arms control and disarmament effort falls into four broad phases:

1945–52: The era of the Baruch Plan and its aftermath in the period of the American nuclear monopoly and the beginning of a Soviet nuclear force.

1953–60: The era of assessment by the post-Stalin leadership in the Soviet Union and by the Eisenhower Administration in the United States, when both nations plunged forward with their respective nuclear developments.

1961–67: The era of limited agreements, chiefly after the Soviet-American confrontation at the nuclear brink over Cuba, after which the Soviet Union rushed to reach at least nuclear parity with the United States.

1968–70: The era when the two superpowers, finding themselves in rough nuclear parity but with new developments threatening to upset what Winston Churchill had popularized as the "delicate balance of terror," warily circled each other and finally agreed to try negotiating about control of the most critical weapons each possessed.

In the quarter-century since the first atomic bomb exploded, both the nuclear arms race and the effort to control it have achieved lives of their own. Technological developments have forced endless changes in political negotiating positions, but it is still a fact that no nuclear weapon has been exploded in anger since Hiroshima and Nagasaki in 1945.

The 1962 Cuban missile crisis led Nikita Khrushchev to remark, when it was over, that "there was a smell of burning in the air." However, it was widely said at the time that both the superpowers had learned something of crisis control. The Moscow-Washington use of the hot line during the Arab-Israeli Six Day War in 1967 showed a mutual sense of restraint.

But weapons development has raced on, the delicate balance of terror has been shaken, if not upset, and new possibilities of nuclear war, including a contest between the Soviet Union and China, have emerged. Efforts to control the nuclear arms race remain inescapable for both the United States and the Soviet Union.

Over the years, the Kremlin has had at its command a group of men both skilled in negotiations and increasingly well informed in arms control problems. Since 1946, when Andrei Gromyko made the first Russian response to Baruch's appeal, only seven men have been the chief negotiators for Russia, and they have been well backstopped at the conference table.

In contrast, U.S. expertise has waxed and waned. There have been three high points: the early Baruch period, the era when Harold Stassen was Eisenhower's disarmament man, and the period since the Arms Control and Disarmament Agency was created by President John F. Kennedy. The American personnel turnover, in part due to changes in administrations, has been far greater than that of the Soviet Union.

In the end, although it is the experts who provide the formulas, it is the political chiefs who make agreement possible. What is critical, therefore, is, on the one hand, a President's dedication, and, on the other, the determination of at least a Kremlin majority.

One striking factor in the history of the nuclear years is how much the political men who make the decisions about such negotiations are not only beholden to, but also captives of, the scientists and technicians who expand nuclear knowledge. Each new weapons development has made it more difficult to find a politically propitious moment to forge an agreement. The problem in arms control is to find that rare moment when, in William C. Foster's words, "the technological stars and planets" are "in favorable conjunction, so to speak"—and are matched to a workable degree by a conjunction of Soviet-American interests in the political sphere.

There has been from the beginning of the nuclear age, and there is today, what Robert S. McNamara, when he was Secretary of Defense, called the "action-reaction phenomenon which fuels the arms race." By that he meant that what one side does in weapons development, out of sheer inventive genius, out of fear of the other nation's development, or out of ignorance of such developments, tends to make the second side react. That this phenomenon is recognized in Moscow as well as in Washington can be seen from the words of Soviet Premier Alexei Kosygin: "The United States must realize that in both physics and politics each action causes a corresponding counteraction."

Both McNamara and Kosygin might have added that the action-reaction phenomenon is expressed in political terms as well as in weapons development. It has never been possible to isolate arms control from the international political environment, especially from the mood of Soviet-American relations.

It is because of such action-reaction that the following account is replete with offer and rejection, proposal and counterproposal, thrust and parry, both in serious effort and in propaganda intent. Positions long and stubbornly held have been suddenly reversed and well-meant offers have been altered or withdrawn, all because of some new action-reaction in the realm of weapons development or in the field of international political relationships.

A second factor of great importance that runs through the history of arms control efforts is the internal dispute over the issue within the government in Washington and, similarly, within the Kremlin.

American Presidents, once in office, find the role of nuclear peacemaker irresistible. But they also find that the men who work for them and with them are often bitterly divided on how to achieve that end—especially in trying to judge the risks involved in any form of nuclear arms control. This has been true in the Truman, Eisenhower, Kennedy, Johnson, and Nixon administrations. Far less is known about what goes on in the Kremlin than about what happens in the American Government. But enough is known to say with certainty that there have been, and probably are today, counterpart disagreements in the Soviet hierarchy. In addition, Soviet decision-making has been seriously affected by rival views on the central issue of whether to deal generally with the United States even before confronting the problem of any particular arms control proposal, and, if so, how.

Both the United States and the Soviet Union in recent years have had their influence in areas outside their own boundaries greatly eroded, even though they remain supreme in the field of nuclear weapons. No government in Washington or Moscow will take very much of a risk, as the record demonstrates. Each has a fear of the unknown and finds it easier to stand pat. Yet each is driven by economic pressures and by ever-recurring glimpses of the nuclear sword of Damocles to try and try again for some new agreement to curb the arms race.

Each President and each Kremlin leader has had to accept the fact, as J. Robert Oppenheimer once put it, that the two superpowers "may be likened to two scorpions in a bottle, each capable of killing the other, but only at the risk of his own life." Abandonment of efforts to control the already terrifying conventional arms race became unthinkable once the Soviet Union as well as the United States had nuclear weapons. Now five nations have nuclear weapons and more are capable of making them. And the scientists, who do not wait for the political leaders, have already moved the arms race into a new, more deadly, and more expensive stage by the development of rival multiple warhead systems for intercontinental ballistic missiles (known by the acronym MIRV) and by creation of rival systems for anti-ballistic-missile defense (ABM).

Because of what this could mean for the safety, perhaps even the survival, of the Soviet Union and the United States, the two superpowers have at long last begun to discuss how they might limit, control, and possibly reduce both offensive and defensive strategic nuclear arms.

What makes two governments keep trying to reach agreements to limit the nuclear arms race? The answer can only be the sheer terror of nuclear war. In 1950, the man whose formula $(E = mc^2)$ first made the bomb possible, Albert Einstein, appeared on American television to discuss the decision to produce the hydrogen bomb. He said:

> If these efforts should prove successful, radioactive poisoning of the atmosphere, and, hence, annihilation of all life on earth, will have been brought within the range of what is technically possible.
>
> A weird aspect of this development lies in its apparently inexorable character. Each step appears as the inevitable consequence of the one that went before.
>
> And at the end, looming ever clearer, lies general annihilation.

The end foreseen by Einstein has not yet arrived. Men in both Washington and Moscow are still trying to see that it does not.

The cynics and the discouraged will say that little or nothing has been accomplished in a quarter-century of effort and thus nothing of substance can now be expected. It is true that what has been arrived at is only a series of essentially peripheral agreements. But it also is true that what is being discussed at the strategic arms limitation talks, for the first time with any real seriousness, goes to the heart of the arms race.

I. The Baruch Plan Era

> I consider the problem of our satisfactory relations with Russia as not merely connected with but as virtually dominated by the problem of the atomic bomb.
> *Secretary of War* HENRY L. STIMSON
> *September 11, 1945*

On a March day in 1945, Senator Arthur H. Vandenberg, the Michigan Republican who was an important minority member of the Senate Foreign Relations Committee, sat beside the cluttered White House desk of President Franklin D. Roosevelt. He spotted on the desk a copy of his own January 10 Senate speech, with a heavy line drawn under the words "If World War III unhappily arrives, it will open new laboratories of death too horrible to contemplate."

The President, seeing that Vandenberg had noted the underlining, gestured toward the manuscript of the speech and remarked, "Senator, you have no idea how right you are, but I think you'll discover before the year is over." Roosevelt had returned the month before from the Yalta Conference with Joseph Stalin and Winston Churchill. Already a sick man, he was to die a month later, but, at the time of his conversation with Vandenberg, he had begun to create what came to be the United Nations. In his thinking, the possibility and the meaning of an atomic bomb had become a critical factor in the future peace of the world.

The first test of an atomic bomb took place in secrecy at Alamogordo, New Mexico, on July 16, 1945. The first bomb exploded in war fell from the bomb bay of a B-29 on Hiroshima, Japan, on August 6, and the second, on Nagasaki, three days later.

Scientifically, the bomb was based on the phenomenon of nuclear fission, which had been universally known since 1939. Soviet scientists were among those who recognized the possibility of the nuclear chain reaction, although the Soviet effort, we now know, did not get under way until 1942. In the United States, several scientists, chiefly refugees from Nazism, worried that German scientists would provide Hitler with an atomic bomb, and so set about to induce President Roosevelt to build such a weapon first. A letter, drafted by Leo Szilard, dated August 2, 1939, and signed by Albert Einstein, himself a refugee in the United States, was sent to FDR, suggesting the possibility of an atomic bomb. This letter, after some delay, led to the creation of the supersecret, multibillion-dollar Manhattan Project, out of which came the world's first nuclear weapons.

When FDR died, one of his Cabinet members, Henry L. Stimson, stayed on for some months to help the new President, Harry S. Truman. Senior statesman Stimson had been Herbert Hoover's Secretary of State and was Roosevelt's Secretary of War during World War II. He prepared a memorandum on the atomic bomb and its relations to foreign policy, which led President Truman, once Japan had surrendered on August 14, 1945, to begin a search for ways to harness this newfound power. The Stimson memorandum was first discussed by Truman's Cabinet on September 11, 1945, the last meeting Stimson attended before he retired from public life.

Stimson clearly saw what lay ahead, as evidenced by a passage from his memorandum:

Those relations [with the Russians] may be perhaps irretrievably embittered by the way in which we approach the solution of the bomb with Russia. For if we fail to approach them now and merely continue to negotiate with them, having this weapon rather ostentatiously on our hip, their suspicions and their distrust of our purposes and motives will increase.

Stimson was pleading for direct Soviet-American discussions, excluding other nations, with the possible exception of Great Britain. It should be recalled that the United States and the Soviet Union had been wartime allies, albeit at times wary of one another and that the majority of Americans, though far from all, devoutly hoped that this relationship would continue after the end of World War II.

But political differences such as that over the fate of Poland had begun to embitter Soviet-American relations in the final weeks of FDR's life, and Truman's impatience with Moscow was evident soon after he became President. At the Potsdam Conference in July, 1945, Truman had hinted to Stalin of the success of the Alamogordo test, word of which reached the President during the meeting. On his return from Potsdam and after the bomb had been dropped on Hiroshima, the President, in a report to the nation, declared:

> The atomic bomb is too dangerous to be loose in a lawless world. That is why Great Britain and the United States, who have the secret of its production, do not intend to reveal the secret until means have been found to control the bomb so as to protect ourselves and the rest of the world from the danger of total destruction.

The news of the achievement of nuclear fission burst for the first time upon all but a handful of people on August 6, 1945, the day the bomb fell on Hiroshima. On August 16, the War Department made public what amounted to a primer on the principles of the process that had made the bomb possible. This was the Smyth Report, named for its author, physicist Henry D. Smyth, who had helped make the bomb and was then serving as a member of the Atomic Energy Commission (he is currently U.S. representative to the International Atomic Energy Agency in Vienna). The problem of the bomb and what to do about it became a matter of wide public discussion, in and out of Congress and the White House.

Stories appeared saying that Truman wanted to share the bomb with the Russians. An argument began over whether the wartime Manhattan Project, which had created the bomb, should now be placed under civilian or military control. Senator Vandenberg called for the creation of what became the Joint Committee on Atomic Energy; it remains today a major power center in the United States on atomic matters.

At the insistence of British Prime Minister Clement Atlee, who had taken over from Churchill in the midst of the Potsdam Conference, a tripartite meeting of Truman, Atlee, and W. L. Mackenzie King of Canada was held in Washington in November. Both the Canadian and the British governments had been associated with the Manhattan Project.

At the conclusion of the meeting, the three leaders produced a declaration of their willingness, as representatives of the only nations then possessing "the knowledge essential to the use of atomic energy [to] proceed with the exchange of fundamental scientific literature for peaceful ends with any nation that will fully reciprocate." But to do so, the statement went on, would be perilous unless "it is possible to devise effective reciprocal and enforceable safeguards acceptable to all nations [which] would contribute to a constructive solution of the problem of the atomic bomb."

In Moscow on December 27, 1945, the Soviet Union agreed with the United States and Great Britain to recommend that the newly created U.N. General Assembly establish a commission "to consider problems arising from the discovery of atomic energy and related matters." The establishing resolution called on the proposed commission, among other things, to come up with proposals "for the elimination from national armaments of atomic and of all other major weapons adaptable to mass destruction" and for effective safeguards against "the hazards of violations and evasions." At Soviet insistence, the resolution also stated that the

Security Council, where the Russians had a veto, should be the U.N. body to "issue directives" to the proposed commission, and that the commission should be accountable to it. It was the Soviet Union's first move to protect its own interests in this new age of atomic weapons.

The tripartite declaration and the establishment of the U.N. Disarmament Commission put pressure on the Truman Administration to come up with a plan quickly. The September 21 Cabinet meeting, at which the Stimson Memorandum was discussed, had gotten nowhere. As Dean Acheson, then Under Secretary of State, said in his memoirs, *Present at the Creation,* "The discussion was unworthy of the subject. No one had had a chance to prepare for its complexities." As acting Secretary of State at the time, Acheson was aware of the problems: the internal American struggle, now clearly visible, over civilian versus military control of atomic energy and the need for an American international position in the wake of the Stimson Memorandum.

The domestic issue was resolved in favor of civilian control. President Truman signed the McMahon Act, named for Senator Brian McMahon, a Connecticut Democrat, August 1, 1946, and thus created the civilian Atomic Energy Commission (AEC), which continues to this day to oversee the production of nuclear material for weapons and for peaceful uses.

The international issue was less successfully resolved. On October 26, 1945, Vandenberg wrote in his diary, later published in *The Private Papers of Senator Vandenberg:*

I am frank to say that I do not yet know what the answer is to the awful problem which we have brought upon ourselves. It seems perfectly clear that we could not hope to monopolize this secret very long. It also seems clear that atomic energy will have to be put under ultimate international control. This would obviously require a complete and absolute right of world-wide inspection and information. It would be unthinkable, for example, for us to voluntarily permit Russia to take the secret of atomic energy behind its blackout curtain to do with it whatever Moscow pleases. . . . I sometimes wonder whether the wit of man is competent to deal with this murderous discovery.

In such a frame of mind, Vandenberg, McMahon, then chairman of the new Joint Committee on Atomic Energy, and others went to see Truman in December. They were alarmed that the new Secretary of State, James F. Byrnes, an ex-senator himself, was going to Moscow to arrange for an exchange of atomic scientists and scientific information without providing for adequate safeguards. The senators insisted on an "ironclad agreement on inspection" and Byrnes's intentions, never fully disclosed, were blocked.

In December, 1945, Byrnes named Dean Acheson to head a committee to work out a plan for the control of nuclear power, to be submitted to the new U.N. Atomic Energy Commission. A board of consultants was headed by David E. Lilienthal, then chairman of the Tennessee Valley Authority and later the first chairman of the U.S. Atomic Energy Commission. Serving with Acheson were Dr. Vannevar Bush, president of the Carnegie Institution and former director of the wartime Office of Scientific Research and Development; Dr. James B. Conant, President of Harvard University; General Leslie R. Groves, who had commanded the Manhattan Project; and John J. McCloy, former Assistant Secretary of War under Stimson. According to Acheson, "the most stimulating and creative mind" in the consultant group was that of J. Robert Oppenheimer, who had headed the project to build the bomb—and who was later, in one of the most celebrated cases of the nuclear quarter century, to have his security clearance revoked.

The committee and its consultants worked until March 28, 1946, to produce their plan, the Acheson-Lilienthal Report. Some of the flavor of the days (and nights) of labor expended on the report have been preserved in an article in *The New Yorker* of August 17, 1946, by Daniel Lang—based on an interview with

Herbert L. Marks, who was Acheson's assistant in the preparation of the report:

> Last winter, a group of seven men made a strong bid for an endurance record of a very special sort when they spent two months talking about nothing but atomic energy and how to control it. . . . The study was a peculiar one because the consultants had little idea of where to start and were even more uncertain about where they were going. . . . The consultants talked atomic energy in Pullman compartments and aloft in an Army plane. Sometimes they deliberated for as long as eighteen hours a day.

These labors ended with four all-day meetings on March 7, 8, 16, and 17, at Dumbarton Oaks, the mansion in Washington, D.C., where the charter of the United Nations had been drafted. In a radio address, Acheson and Bush discussed the report, which proposed "a plan under which no nation would make atomic bombs or the materials for them. All dangerous activities would be carried on—not merely inspected—by a live, functioning international authority with a real purpose in the world and capable of attracting competent personnel." The current monopoly enjoyed by the United States, they went on to say, "is only temporary. It will not last. We must use that advantage now to promote international security and to carry out our policy of building a lasting peace through international agreement."

When Acheson turned the plan over to Byrnes, the Secretary of State told him he would recommend to Truman that Bernard M. Baruch be appointed to turn the proposals "into a workable plan" and to present the plan to the United Nations. Acheson protested. He felt, as he later wrote, that Baruch, long called adviser to Presidents, since he had been just that from the days of the Wilson Administration, was anything but a wise man. Truman, though he accepted Byrnes's recommendation, later resented Baruch's demand for wide authority and wrote that "his concern, in my opinion, was really whether he would receive public recognition." There was much pulling and hauling between Baruch and those who had drafted the Acheson-Lilienthal Report, but the essence of the report was the essence of the Baruch Plan. As it turned out, both were unacceptable to the Soviet Union, and it is now evident that any such scheme was doomed to failure.

What Baruch proposed before the U.N. Disarmament Commission on June 14, 1946, with all the histrionics and prestige that were his to employ, was a system of complete control of the entire process of producing atomic weapons, from the mining of the raw materials, uranium and thorium, to the manufacture of new weapons and, eventually, the disposal of existing ones. This control system was also to apply to the use of nuclear energy for peaceful purposes, such as the generation of electric power.

The plan was to be implemented by an International Atomic Development Authority, which would have exclusive ownership of "all atomic energy activities potentially dangerous to world security." The proposed agency would have worldwide powers of inspection and of sanctions against violators. If the Soviet Union would agree to the scheme, the United States was prepared to hand over to the new agency both the data on which its technical knowledge was based and its stockpile of atomic weapons.

The Acheson-Lilienthal Report had proposed no scheme of sanctions to punish violators. Baruch had seized on this point, insisting, as Secretary Byrnes related in *Speaking Frankly*, that any violator (the presumption, of course, was that the violator, if any, would be the Soviet Union) "should be subjected to swift and sure punishment; and in case of violation no one of the permanent members of the Security Council should be permitted to veto punitive action by the council." Truman approved, and thus the proposal for sanctions by a majority vote of the Security Council became a part of the Baruch Plan.

To the Americans who had labored so long and hard to create a plan to beat the nuclear sword into a plowshare, the offer, even with the sanction provision, seemed most generous; indeed, there were many who objected that it was far too generous. But the Baruch Plan suffered one fatal flaw: it was founded on a misreading of Stalin's Soviet Union of 1946. To the plan's authors, the scheme was a rational proposal that rational men surely ought to accept, and the authors had high hopes that this would be the case in Moscow. But the bomb had upset the balance of power achieved by the end of World War II between the Red Army and the forces of the Western Allies. Hence, to Stalin the Baruch Plan was nothing more than an American attempt to impose on the world a nuclear Pax Americana, a device to relegate the Soviet Union forever to second-class status. Stalin saw no generous offer; rather he probably suspected that, in the end, the United States would not really relinquish its atomic weapons but would manage to force the Soviet Union to submit to international inspection, thus laying bare the terrible weaknesses of postwar Russia, and to fasten upon the world American control of the authority to exploit, and reap the profits of, the peaceful atom.

In a 1962 interview with a group of visiting American journalists, Nikita Khrushchev gave just such a retrospective Soviet view. He said the aim of the Baruch Plan was

> to set up an international control organ, which would enjoy the right of ownership of atomic raw materials and atomic plants, the right of control over all research in the sphere of atomic energy, the right to interfere in the economic life of nations. This is what the United States strove for, and not to ban nuclear weapons or to destroy them. It wanted to prevent the development of the atomic industry in other countries, leaving the monopoly of nuclear arms to the United States. We, of course, could not agree to this.

Furthermore, said Khrushchev, "What would it have meant to put the development of atomic energy under U.N. control? That would have meant to put it under control of the U.S. inasmuch as the U.N., in point of fact, is a branch of the U.S. Department of State."

In their idealistic hopes of controlling the atom, few Americans viewed the problem from the Kremlin's standpoint. What Stalin saw in the Baruch Plan was a totally one-sided, and therefore unacceptable, proposal.

But in 1946 the world was weary of war and frightened at the monstrous blows inflicted on Hiroshima and Nagasaki only a few months earlier. There was then none of the Khrushchevian blunt talk. Instead, Stalin's response represented neither direct confrontation nor outright rejection but counterproposal and obfuscation—moves designed to play for time. American action had produced Soviet reaction.

It is important to remember that in the year following the end of World War II, Stalin's postwar foreign policy was slowly becoming apparent, although there were many in the West, especially in the United States, who did their best not to believe what they saw because of what it presaged.

W. Averell Harriman, wartime ambassador in Moscow, said many years later, "When I saw Stalin himself, at Sochi, in October, 1945, he said 'We have decided to go our own way.'" According to Harriman, Stalin believed that, with Europe prostrate, "there could be a Communist takeover in Western Europe," including France, Italy, and Germany. Many historians now doubt any such intentions on Stalin's part, given his immense problems at home in recovering from the devastation caused by Hitler's armies, but at the time there was widespread fear of a Russian invasion of Western Europe.

Stalin himself, in a speech on February 9, 1946, which appeared to be stating a policy along the lines of his remark to Harriman, took a classical Marxist view of the war:

> The war was the inevitable result of the development of world economic and political forces on the basis of modern monopoly capitalism. Marxists have declared more than once that the capitalist system of world economy harbors elements of general crises and armed conflicts and that, hence, the development of world capitalism in our time proceeds not in the form of smooth and even progress but through crises and military catastrophes.

Against this view, and his economists' predictions of a shattering American economic depression, Stalin, in his speech, called for organizing "a new mighty upsurge for the national economy, which would allow us to increase our industrial production, for example, three times over as compared with the prewar period. . . . Only under such conditions can we consider that our homeland will be guaranteed against all possible accidents."

This was disturbing news for official Washington; it was a renunciation of the wartime alliance with the United States and Britain against Hitler's Germany. It was not a view of the world in which any such scheme as the Baruch Plan could have a place. The origin of the Cold War has often been dated from Stalin's speech. (It came a month before Winston Churchill, in Fulton, Missouri, with President Truman beside him, charged that an "iron curtain" had descended in Europe, dividing East from West.) But whatever the origins of the Cold War (a matter recently raised by the so-called revisionist historians), it was and, in many respects, remains today a fact of international life. What is important here is how it influenced the actions of the United States and the Soviet Union in arms control matters.

Thus, it is not surprising, in retrospect, that only five days after Baruch's sonorous presentation of "a choice between the quick and the dead," his Soviet counterpart replied with a plan that would have annulled the atomic monopoly of the United States. Andrei Gromyko, then Moscow's Security Council representative and a deputy foreign minister (and since 1957, the foreign minister for successive Kremlin regimes), called for an international convention "prohibiting the production and employment of weapons based on the use of atomic energy." Those who signed the convention were to agree "not to use atomic weapons in any circumstances whatsoever; to prohibit the production and storing of weapons based on the use of atomic energy; to destroy, within a period of three months . . . all stocks of atomic energy weapons whether in a finished or unfinished condition."

The Soviet Union had posed the central conundrum of many

nuclear control measures: Which comes first—the commitments to disarm or the measures to ensure the observance of commitments? (as Bechhoefer succinctly put it in *Postwar Negotiations for Arms Control*).

It should be remembered that the United States rapidly demobilized its armed forces soon after the end of World War II, thus leaving the A-bomb as the chief American deterrent against any attack across Europe by what was believed to be a vast Red Army. (At that time, Western intelligence, as to both Soviet military manpower and Soviet intentions, was far inferior to what it later became.)

On August 6, Gromyko gave the *coup de grâce* to the Baruch Plan when he said that the inspection proposed by Baruch was not reconcilable with the principle of national sovereignty. This statement had been foreshadowed by remarks of Gromyko to Baruch, related to Lilienthal, who recorded them in his journal. On July 28, Baruch told Lilienthal that "Gromyko understands about the veto, etc., but that his real objection isn't the veto but rather the whole idea of permitting their country to be subjected to inspection from without."

The thinking that lay behind the Kremlin proposal of what was a simple "ban the bomb" convention was quite specifically set out in 1963 during an exchange of polemics between Moscow and Peking. An official Soviet statement contained this candid account of what had been in the Kremlin's mind in 1946:

In the early years after the United States developed nuclear weapons, when the U.S. had a nuclear monopoly and the security of the socialist [Communist] countries was thus endangered, the Soviet Government proceeded from the consideration that the main thing was to deprive the U.S. of this advantage. That could be achieved either through a complete ban on nuclear weapons which would have been tantamount to taking them away from the only nuclear power of the day, the United States; or through developing nuclear weapons of our own which would serve to protect the security of all the socialist countries.

In fact, the Soviet Union worked both lines of that approach. In the propaganda field, Moscow played on fears of another war by promoting U.N. resolutions similar in tone to one condemning "the preparations for a new war being conducted in a number of countries and particularly in the United States and in the United Kingdom." This propaganda drive reached its peak in the March, 1950 World Congress of Partisans of Peace, which produced the Stockholm Appeal demanding "the absolute banning of the atom weapon. . . ." Literally millions around the world signed the appeal.

Privately, the Soviet scientists whom Stalin had first put to work in 1942 continued their secret effort to break the American monopoly on nuclear weapons. There is no doubt that Soviet espionage helped the effort. Klaus Fuchs, the German-born British scientist who transmitted secrets to Moscow, was among those officially present when the Nuclear Age began at Alamogordo, New Mexico, in 1945. There were others, too, whose feats of espionage were surely of help.

Publicly, Stalin deprecated the bomb. In 1946, he said that "atomic bombs are intended to frighten people with weak nerves, but they cannot decide the outcome of a war since for this atomic bombs are completely insufficient." But the next year, in private, he told Yugoslavia's Milovan Djilas that the bomb "is a powerful thing, pow-er-ful!" What was really in the Soviet mind was more candidly stated in 1945 by Foreign Minister V. M. Molotov, who declared that "it is not possible . . . for a technical secret of any great size to remain the exclusive possession of one country. . . . We will have atomic energy and many other things, too."

The Soviet effort culminated in a nuclear explosion on August 23, 1949, three years and two months after the Baruch Plan had been proposed and years before the date predicted by most American estimates. It was a long time, however, before Moscow felt it had nuclear weapons enough to deter Washington and to create, through a near parity in nuclear weapons, an atmosphere in which negotiations to curb the arms race might be feasible.

By the time of the initial Soviet test, the Cold War was on in earnest. Europe had truly divided East from West. Churchill's iron curtain was a reality, and the Berlin blockade had already provided a test of strength. The United States had begun the Marshall Plan to rescue Western Europe, by reviving it economically, from the threat of Communism, and President Truman had proclaimed the doctrine that "it must be the policy of the United States to support free peoples who are resisting attempted subjugation by armed minorities or by outright pressures."

The Truman Administration had adopted George Kennan's policy for the "containment" of the Soviet Union. Five days before the first Soviet test, the North Atlantic Treaty came into force, and the organization created by the treaty (NATO) was born. The Korean War soon followed. The United States, fearful of a Soviet attack in Western Europe while it was engaged in Korea, rearmed West Germany and brought the country into NATO. Both events were anathema to the Soviet Union.

There simply was no conjunction of Soviet-American interests to make possible any arms control measures. It is true that on June 11, 1947, Gromyko had somewhat modified the Soviet proposals on treaty safeguards, perhaps a sign, as some in Washington said, of a victory for more moderate elements in the Kremlin. At any rate, neither these concessions nor any of the lengthy discussions at the United Nations produced anything remotely resembling agreement between the two nations. The aims of Moscow and Washington were too divergent and their nuclear disparity far too great to permit agreement. Byrnes said in 1947 that the United States sought "collective security," whereas the Soviet Union's preference was "for the simpler task of dividing the world into two spheres of influence." So it seemed to the American Government.

Thus, the Baruch Plan, in which so much effort and so much

hope had been invested, was doomed from the day it was put forward.

Truman was instantly suspicious of the Soviet refusal to agree to verification, and he wrote to Baruch, "We should not under any circumstances throw away our gun until we are sure the rest of the world can't arm against us." The U.N. Disarmament Commission did, in time, adopt what was substantially the American proposal, but the gesture was meaningless since both the Soviet Union and Poland voted against the proposal, and, when the commission report was sent to the Security Council, the Soviet veto blocked all action.

The British, meanwhile, had been cut off from American nuclear information, despite what both London and Ottawa considered a binding agreement to continue the wartime cooperation. Along with creating the Atomic Energy Commission, the McMahon Act barred the executive branch from giving any nation information that would help it build nuclear weapons. The British subsequently went into the nuclear weapons business on their own. After the initial British successes, Congress amended the McMahon Act to permit American aid to go to those nations the President found had "made substantial progress in the development of atomic weapons." This allowed President Eisenhower to aid the British. President Kennedy later said publicly that France also technically met the requirement, but neither he nor his successors granted such aid to France because of Franco-American political differences arising from President Charles de Gaulle's hostility toward NATO.

Baruch himself resigned after a few months, once it was evident no agreement with the Soviet Union was likely. His plan, however, remained the centerpiece of American nuclear disarmament policy for nine more years, well into the Eisenhower Administration.

The American discovery, by aerial sampling off Japan, that the Soviets had achieved an atomic explosion (announced shortly thereafter by President Truman) produced a major internal, and

—from *The Herblock Book* (Beacon Press, 1952)

highly secret, American debate over whether the United States should proceed to develop a thermonuclear weapon, as the H-bomb is correctly called. The principle behind such a weapon was known in the scientific world, but there were grave doubts about the possibility of its development, although modest research had gone on ever since Hiroshima had definitely proved the feasibility of the A-bomb.

The H-bomb offered a quantum jump in explosive power, but in the period of the American monopoly of the A-bomb, it had seemed superfluous. Indeed, the military had developed no requirement for it at all. But action-reaction came into play with the news of the first Soviet A-bomb test.

There ensued a bitter controversy in the American Government, in which Oppenheimer, as chairman of the Atomic Energy Commission's General Advisory Committee, was to play a major role. It was his opposition to development of the H-bomb that led to the official revoking of his security clearance at the termination of what eventually became known as the Oppenheimer case. The H-bomb debate, both in secret and, after President Truman ordered a go-ahead, in public, centered on whether such a weapon was needed, the morality of its manufacture, and the effect its development would have on relations with the Soviet Union. One of the leading proponents of H-bomb development was Lewis Strauss, then a member (and later chairman) of the Atomic Energy Commission. He favored building the bomb by a crash program if necessary to "stay ahead" of Soviet nuclear development. On Strauss's side was physicist Edward Teller, who later provided some of the key formulas that resulted in success.

But others in both the scientific and political communities in the United States wanted to try first for an agreement with the Soviet Union to avoid this jump in weaponry. One of them was Henry D. Smyth, another was the physicist Lee DuBridge, then President of the California Institute of Technology (and now President Nixon's science adviser at the White House).

On January 27, 1950, the British informed the United States

of the arrest of Klaus Fuchs, who confessed to atomic espionage. Four days later, Secretary of State Acheson and Secretary of Defense Louis Johnson told the President he should go ahead with the development of the H-bomb, but Lilienthal, then chairman of the Atomic Energy Commission, was opposed. On January 31, the President announced his decision. The bomb was to be developed. Once again, Soviet action had produced American reaction. The Strauss theme that the United States must "stay ahead" was clearly dominant in the American mood, both in and out of the Administration and in the Congress.

In the final Truman years, the government was on the defensive. Senator Joseph R. McCarthy, the Wisconsin Republican, had begun to make his spies-in-government charges and to conduct a related campaign against Acheson. The British were embarrassed by the arrest of Fuchs and his confessions of espionage. In 1951, as Acheson has recently related, the British asked the United States to test an atomic bomb for them, but the Administration was so diffident in its relations with Congress that it would not risk even asking for congressional approval. The beginning of the Korean War in June, 1950, turned the Cold War hot and presented Truman with a more pressing problem than how to continue negotiations on nuclear arms.

The last major action relating to arms control during the Truman period was Acheson's creation of a panel to work out comprehensive plans for control and reduction of both conventional and nuclear arms. Oppenheimer and Bush were both members of the group. Oppenheimer's subsequent remark about the two scorpions in a bottle was reflective of his pessimism, especially since work on the H-bomb had been expedited. (Oppenheimer, incidentally, had borrowed the famous simile from Bush, who had used it in an earlier speech.)

This final arms control effort of the Truman years led Bush to suggest an understanding with the Soviet Union that neither nation would detonate an H-bomb, even if they had developed it to the point of testing. This was the germ of the test ban treaty that was to come to fulfillment only during the Kennedy Administration. But Bush's proposal was vetoed by the panel on which he served. It is highly doubtful that in its final months the Truman Administration would have had sufficient authority, so low by then was it in public esteem, to make such a proposal public. At any rate, it did not, and the next moves in the nuclear field were left to the Administration's successor.

II. Time of Assessment

> Since the advent of nuclear weapons, it
> seems clear that there is no longer any
> alternative to peace, if there is to be a
> happy and well world.
> *President* DWIGHT D. EISENHOWER
> *October 19, 1954*

General Dwight D. Eisenhower entered the White
House on January 20, and Joseph Stalin died on March 6, 1953.
These two events produced re-examinations in both capitals,
which, however, did not begin to be reflected at the conference
table for another two years and were not fully reflected until
1957.

When the two nations were finally prepared to negotiate, it
was against a different backdrop from that of the Baruch era, for
the world had moved from the atomic age to the thermonuclear
age. The first experimental American hydrogen bomb device had
been exploded on November 1, 1952, three days before Eisenhower was elected President. The first Soviet H-bomb test came
nine months later.

In the Soviet Union, post-Stalin debate on nuclear problems
appears to have begun early in 1954. It was intertwined with the
struggle for power in the Kremlin.

On March 12, 1954, Premier Georgi Malenkov declared that
a third world war "with the existence of the modern means of
destruction would mean the destruction of world civilization."

This deviation from the Leninist doctrine of the inevitability of a "frightful conflict" between Communist and capitalist states undoubtedly reflected discussions on the meaning of thermonuclear weapons and on the desirability of coming to terms with the United States.

But on February 8, 1955, Malenkov "resigned," and Foreign Minister Molotov thereupon publicly repudiated the Malenkov doctrine by saying that "what will perish" in a new war "will not be world civilization, however much it may suffer from new aggression," but the "rotten social systems" of the capitalist nations.

This critical difference in doctrinal view does not appear to have been resolved until Nikita Khrushchev's assumption of first place in the Kremlin hierarchy and his 1956 pronouncement at the Twentieth Communist Party Congress that "there is no fatal inevitability of war." Concurrent with this change was the increasing stress that Moscow placed on "peaceful coexistence" between capitalist and Communist nations. Lenin had created the peaceful coexistence theme in a time of dire necessity, but it had fallen into disuse in the period of Stalin's hostility to the West.

Khrushchev was adept at finding ideological cover for pragmatic facts. His stress on peaceful coexistence was born of necessity, a necessity he recognized in 1960 when he said in a speech that the use of nuclear weapons "would not distinguish between Communists and non-Communists, between atheists and believers, between Catholics and Protestants." By 1963, after the Cuban missile crisis with the United States and the open break with China, the Soviet Communist Party adopted the Khrushchevian logic by formally declaring, in an attempt to differentiate between Soviet and Chinese policies, that "the atomic bomb does not adhere to the class principle—it destroys everybody within the range of its devastating force."

It is now apparent that the Soviet Union moved more slowly than did the United States to an appreciation of the meaning of the nuclear age and of the necessity for control of the new weapons. On assuming office, Eisenhower had made a review of the nuclear arms race and was alarmed at what he found. Seeking a positive rather than a negative approach, he had rejected a plan (dubbed "Operation Candor") to make public the grim facts about the effects of a nuclear war and instead made his famous "Atoms for Peace" speech on December 8, 1953. In it, he offered the thesis that to develop the peaceful atom would be a step toward diminishing "the potential destructiveness of the world's atomic stockpiles."

But the atoms for peace approach was no substitute for a full-scale arms control plan.* Not until March 19, 1955, did Eisenhower create the position of Special Assistant to the President for Disarmament—with Cabinet rank—and name Harold Stassen, former governor of Minnesota and then head of the foreign aid program, to fill the post. In August, after a Soviet arms control proposal, the President gave Stassen negotiating as well as planning power.

Eisenhower's appointment of Stassen was evidence of the soldier-President's determination to give serious attention to disarmament. All Presidents in the nuclear age have had added to the innate loneliness of their office the sense of responsibility that springs from their command of the nuclear arsenal. Eisenhower, who had commanded 12 million men in the most destructive war in human history, felt deeply this responsibility from the moment he entered the White House.

---

* Eisenhower's 1953 "Atoms for Peace" speech did lead, however, on July 29, 1957, to creation of the International Atomic Energy Agency (IAEA), a United Nations agency with headquarters in Vienna. Both Washington and Moscow believed that such an organization would prevent the program for the peaceful uses of atomic energy (largely for the generation of electricity) from being used as a cover for the manufacture of atomic weapons among the nations involved in the program. As a gesture of support for the plan, and also in an effort to nudge the Russians into a reciprocal act, Eisenhower in 1956 offered to make available 40,000 kilograms of U-235, the raw material of bombs, for peaceful purposes, chiefly for use in nuclear reactors to generate electricity. The IAEA has come to play a role in this growing field of the peaceful atom, but it has always been a minor aspect of the nuclear arms control problem.

In the second volume of his memoirs, Eisenhower wrote that he often felt he was struggling with both his own advisers and the Russians. Yet, as one who knew firsthand that "war is stupid, cruel, and costly," he also felt that "hope is more difficult to kill than men, and humanity is not ready spinelessly to accept the cynical conclusion that war is certain to recur, that the law of the jungle must forever be the rule of life." And so he sought arms control or at least ways of "reducing the fear of global cataclysm and the practical extinction of civilization."

But in the early Eisenhower years, fear of Communism was very real. The emphasis was on ways to defend the government against it and to prevent its spread. Eisenhower's Secretary of State, John Foster Dulles, was the chief exponent of these efforts. In the diplomatic field, he negotiated a series of treaties that he hoped would contain Communism in the Middle East and Asia, as the NATO treaty had done in Europe. In the military field, he enunciated the doctrine that the United States would rely "primarily on the capacity to retaliate, instantly, by means and at places of its own choosing," whenever there was an attack.

This became known as the "instant massive retaliation doctrine," and it dominated American thinking for most of the Eisenhower era. It was based, in part, on budget limitations, which led to what became known as "more bang for the buck," or less reliance on men in uniform and on conventional weapons and more emphasis on a growing nuclear arsenal. Fundamental to the thesis was a vast American preponderance in nuclear arms, a view that was basic to Dulles's own thinking.

Dulles saw the American mission as born of both this military predominance and an ethical or even religious superiority over the Communist world. Thus he found it impossible intellectually to accept in any sense Soviet-American parity, in arms or in diplomacy. The schism that was to open between him and Stassen sprang from this view.

Dulles's influence with the President was great, for Eisenhower shared many of the Secretary's views. For example, at the end of his second term, Eisenhower concluded that the results of his efforts in the arms control field had been "meager, almost negligible," and that this "failure can be explained in one sentence: It was the adamant insistence of the Communists on maintaining a closed society."

But that was a retrospective and much oversimplified view. In office, Eisenhower sought to find what he called "creative proposals that might, if accepted by others, lead to progress." And he did so, despite Dulles's often dire views of the dangers involved in dealing with the Russians. It was the President's desire at least to try that gave Stassen his opportunities. Soon after Stassen's appointment, for reasons not directly related to arms control, Eisenhower agreed to a summit conference with the Soviet, British, and French leaders. The conference was to provide the setting for the President's major initiative in arms control.

On Thursday afternoon, July 21, 1955, at Geneva, Switzerland, sitting at the huge, square table in the Palais des Nations, President Eisenhower laid his glasses before him, disdaining the prepared manuscript, and began:

> Gentlemen, since I have been working on this memorandum to present to this conference, I have been searching my heart and mind for something that I could say here that could convince everyone of the great sincerity of the United States in approaching this problem of disarmament.

Then, looking directly at Soviet Premier Nikolai Bulganin, Communist Party First Secretary Khrushchev, and Defense Minister Georgi Zhukov, the President went on:

> I should address myself for a moment principally to the delegates from the Soviet Union, because our two great countries admittedly possess new and terrible weapons in quantities which do give rise in other parts of the world, or reciprocally, to the fears and dangers of surprise attack.
>
> I propose, therefore, that we take a practical step, that we begin an arrangement, very quickly, as between ourselves—immediately.

Eisenhower went on to outline an "Open Skies" proposal that called for a swap of both military blueprints and, more importantly, of flights by the planes of one nation across the territory of the other.

In the American mind, the proposal offered assurance against what the United States most feared: a surprise attack or, in the phrase of the time, a nuclear Pearl Harbor. This was the age of the manned bomber armed with nuclear weapons. Open Skies was the American reaction to the growing Soviet nuclear stockpile and the skimpy American knowledge of the Russians' ability to deliver nuclear bombs.

Although there are few revealing Soviet statements on what was then in Moscow's mind, it is not difficult to guess. On the same day the plan was presented, Khrushchev told Eisenhower that the idea was nothing more than a bold espionage plot against the Soviet Union.

From the American standpoint, Open Skies was an effort to break down, by agreement, the age-old Russian suspicion of the foreigner in (and now over) his land. After Russia became the Union of Soviet Socialist Republics, secrecy came to have a dual function. It protected Soviet military and political secrets, and it at the same time concealed Soviet economic weaknesses. But Soviet secrecy in the face of America's relative openness provided an asymmetrical advantage for the Kremlin; secrecy, plus the weapons the Soviets possessed, balanced the larger American nuclear force.

Thus, to Khrushchev in 1955, it appeared that Eisenhower was trying to rip away this advantage, whatever then may have been the degree of Soviet fear of a possible American nuclear first strike. To the President, it was Soviet obstinacy over the inspection issue, an attitude he ascribed to "fear that once they lifted the Iron Curtain their own people, discovering the goodness and richness of life in freedom, might repudiate Communism itself, and, learning of the sincerely peaceful intentions of free peoples who had been proclaimed to them as deadly enemies, would soon reject the Communist goal of world domination."

Eisenhower's assumption is not repeated here because it was correct (it was, indeed, far to simplistic,) but because it illuminates the Soviet-American gulf in the Eisenhower era and demonstrates how little most of those in Washington understood Soviet motivation in dealing with nuclear arms control issues.

Open Skies failed because, as with the Baruch Plan, there existed neither a conjunction of political interests nor the equally necessary balance of military power to make agreement possible. The ideological gulf, of course, made the problem more difficult, but, as later agreements have demonstrated, the United States and the Soviet Union can ignore the gulf, if not put it out of mind, when each decides that an agreement is mutually advantageous.

Open Skies remained an official American offer long after there was any chance of its acceptance. It served, too, to gain points for the United States in the Moscow-Washington propaganda war, for it was an immensely popular conception in many parts of the world, whatever the experts and government leaders may have thought of its practicality.

One factor that had led Eisenhower to his Open Skies offer was a proposal by the Russians some two months earlier. From the American viewpoint, the first reflection of new thinking in the Kremlin came on May 10, 1955, when Soviet representatives, at a subcommittee meeting at the U.N. Disarmament Commission, unexpectedly offered what the West took to be the first serious Soviet effort to deal with both nuclear and conventional weapons. The Soviet document declared that "science and engineering" had produced "the most destructive means of annihilating people," a phrase that appeared to compromise the Malenkov-Molotov gap. The May 10 proposal had three key features: (1) It divided the proposed total disarmament process into stages in place of the previous insistence that everything occur at once; (2) it proposed an end to nuclear tests with a vague international supervision; and (3) it proposed for the first time that foreign control personnel be stationed at "large ports, at railway junctions, on main motor highways and in aerodromes" in the Soviet Union (as well as in other countries) to check the proposed arms control measures. The United States had not expected such a move and was caught unprepared. For almost two years, Stassen worked to evolve, out of conflicting views within the Eisenhower Administration, a response to the proposal that conceivably could produce agreement. Eisenhower himself later wrote that "disarmament was a subject of varying, and often sharply opposing, views among departments and agencies of the United States government and outside them." Open Skies itself had evolved from the work of a group in which Nelson A. Rockefeller, then a Presidential special assistant, played a major role. It was not sold to the top American military and diplomatic officials until the days immediately preceding its enunciation.

It is probable that the worldwide interest in Open Skies lay behind a Soviet decision disclosed in October, 1955, at the Big Four Foreign Ministers Conference in Geneva. Soviet Foreign Minister Molotov announced that his country would accept aerial photography as an inspection technique but only in what he termed "the final stages of carrying out measures directed towards the reduction of armaments and the prohibition of atomic weapons." The foreign ministers meeting, which was chiefly concerned with the problem of Germany, was a failure, but what Khrushchev and others had called "the Spirit of Geneva" continued to exist. Thus, in February, 1956, Khrushchev declared that "for the first time since the war a certain *détente* has set in [in] international tension." He went on to say that, given "equal efforts and mutual concessions" by both sides, the Soviet Union expressed "readiness to agree to certain partial measures," including an end of nuclear testing, prohibition of nuclear weapons on West German soil, and reduction of military budgets.

Khrushchev's words were based on a knowledge of thermonuclear weapons. He called for "peaceful coexistence," declaring there was "no other way out in the present situation. Indeed, there are only two ways: either peaceful coexistence or the most devastating war in history. There is no third alternative."

On May 14, 1956, Moscow announced its intention to reduce its armed forces by 1.2 million men. Khrushchev, reacting to the advent of the H-bomb and to his anticipatory knowledge of intercontinental missiles that would deliver the bomb, determined to trim conventional weapons and manpower. He publicly ridiculed naval vessels other than submarines and extolled strategic weapons when the latter were still in the early stages of development. Many observers believe that he did so in hope of transferring badly needed funds from the military to other sectors of the Soviet economy. Whatever the exact purpose, and despite infighting in the Kremlin in which, at least for a period, Khrushchev's arguments prevailed over the advice of the marshals, there resulted considerable East-West negotiation on military manpower. At one point, there was a tentative Soviet-American agreement that the armed forces of the three great land powers—the United States, the Soviet Union, and Communist China—be set at or reduced to 2.5 million men each, with a quota of 750,000 men for Great Britain and the same for France. Washington was searching for ways to save money and was extolling nuclear weapons at the same time. In 1957, Eisenhower cut the armed forces to a 2.5-million level. But this tentative agreement never reached treaty form because of the inspection and verification issue. To this day, there has been no agreement of any kind on conventional weapons, military manpower, or a combination of the two.

In 1956, the Suez crisis and the Hungarian revolution forced arms control into the shadows, but, by March of the following year, the two sides were ready to try again. From March to November, during meetings of a subcommittee of the U.N. Disarmament Commission in London, both sides put forward new proposals. Serious negotiations got under way on the thesis, basic to Stassen's thinking, that some form of parity-of-risk had to be accepted by the superpowers.

At London, both sides adjusted their proposals in light of their respective examinations of the balance of power in nuclear and conventional arms. Not surprisingly, the United States tried out proposals to trim Soviet strength in conventional arms while the Soviet Union sought to nullify American nuclear power.

In the many proposals and counterproposals of this era, both sides found themselves proposing what they had spurned when the other side had suggested it. This was especially true in attempts to control conventional arms and military manpower. By the time of the 1957 London meeting, however, Soviet nuclear strength had so grown that the key American efforts centered on control of nuclear weapons. More and more, talk of conventional arms and manpower was relegated to the sidelines.

The United States concentrated in this period on limiting and eventually ending nuclear testing while it still had the larger inventory and the more advanced development. It was concerned moreover with methods of protecting itself against a surprise Soviet attack, now that Moscow had produced an H-bomb, and on beginning a cutback in the production of fissionable material for weapons use. (The United States was beginning to have a surplus of such materials.)

The Soviet proposal of May 10, 1955, and the amended proposal of April 30, 1957, reflected a growing nuclear arsenal but one still considerably inferior to that of the United States. It also reflected an important political consideration—Soviet fears that the United States would arm the West Germans with nuclear weapons. The Soviet proposals called for an end to nuclear tests but without inspection (a move that would preserve secrecy), for a renunciation of the use of the bomb long before a cutoff in fissionable material production (a step that would inhibit the use of the superior U.S. Air Force), and for aerial inspection of Europe outside the Soviet Union. This last proposal had the dual virtue, from the Kremlin's standpoint, of offering a means of controlling the growing power of West Germany and of providing a response to Eisenhower's Open Skies offer.

The proposal for aerial inspection of Europe, most specifically of West Germany, raised a storm in Bonn. Chancellor Konrad Adenauer, the good and close friend of John Foster Dulles, had to be reassured that his nation's interests would not be damaged. This reassurance was fatal to Stassen's hopes.

Stassen did manage, after months of intra-Administration and inter-Allied argument, to bring the Open Skies proposal down to negotiable terms. Suggestions came from all sides, but not until August, 1957, was a substantive American plan presented.

Stassen suggested three alternative proposals for aerial inspection, as shown in Appendix II, Map 1. The proposals were for mutual aerial inspection of (a) all of the United States and Canada on the one side and the Soviet Union on the other, roughly the same areas (Alternative 1 on Map 1); (b) an area north of the Arctic Circle that would include parts of the Soviet Union and Canada, with an extension southward to take in all of Alaska (Alternative 2); (c) a pie-shaped wedge of Europe with the North Pole at its point and the Mediterranean Sea as its southern boundary, including most of Western Europe plus the western and most populous part of the Soviet Union (European Zone).

The Soviets had, at first, proposed a European inspection zone, then a zone including about two-thirds of the United States, plus Western Siberia and Alaska (Appendix II, Map 2). The final Soviet proposal, which was not offered until after the breakdown of the London Conference, repeated the Western United States–Siberia–Alaska zone and added Europe, roughly from mid-France to the Soviet border, as well as Greece, Turkey, and Iran, all militarily associated with the United States (Appendix II, Map 3).

In the midst of the London talks, Stassen fell from grace in Washington. The situation, widely reported at the time, undermined the American position by casting doubts on who was speaking for the United States.

During the conference, Stassen had won Eisenhower's approval for what was called a "talking paper," something less firm than a proposal, that included an aerial inspection scheme and a plan to prohibit the use of nuclear weapons except in defense or retaliation in case of nuclear attack. The details were less important than the fact that Stassen foolishly "showed the gist of this paper to the Russians," as Eisenhower later recounted it, "without prior coordination with our allies." The result was trouble with both the British and the Germans.

British Prime Minister Harold Macmillan complained directly to the President that a clause in the Stassen paper that called for devoting future production of fissionable material to peaceful purposes would prevent Britain "from developing the nuclear strength which she is just beginning to acquire." Eisenhower reprimanded Stassen for the "acute embarrassment" Eisenhower felt because the British had not been forewarned, even though, in healing the Anglo-American breach after the Suez crisis, he had pledged fullest future cooperation.

More important, however, was the reaction of Adenauer and Dulles. Alarmed at the Stassen proposals, Adenauer came to Washington to insist that disarmament should come after, not before, the reunification of Germany. His rejection of any German role in a European aerial inspection scheme or in a reduction of conventional weapons confined the London Conference, in essence, to a possible agreement on ending nuclear tests.

Stassen denied he had been reprimanded by the President, but Dulles sent a diplomat to London as Stassen's deputy, an obvious sign of displeasure among many signs evident at the time. Furthermore, Dulles said publicly that the assent of all of the Allies would be necessary for any agreement. And finally, Dulles himself went to the conference to present the Western position. Stassen's usefulness was at an end. He held his post into 1958, but other events by then had altered the Soviet-American relationship in nuclear arms.

In his approach to arms control, Stassen was ahead of his time. He fought within the Eisenhower Administration for acceptance of the thesis that a Soviet Union armed with H-bombs, even though it lacked the arms stockpile and delivery system available

"1945 – 46 – 47 – 48 – 49 – 50 – 51 – 52 – 53 – "

—from *Herblock's Here and Now* (Simon & Schuster, 1955)

to the United States, was a formidable potential foe and therefore should be granted a status of equality in arms control discussions. But in 1957, the uncertainties in Washington about the nature and extent of Soviet nuclear power were many, and those who refused to accept Stassen's parity thesis were powerful. Chief among them was Dulles. As he had fought against the 1955 Geneva Summit Conference because it meant political parity for for Soviet Union with the United States, so he fought against Stassen's thesis of arms control parity on the grounds that the United States was incomparably the more powerful in nuclear weaponry.

Dulles's doctrine of massive retaliation, and the Kremlin's knowledge that the United States had the means to put the doctrine into practice—whatever the Soviet judgment may have been about the American will to employ such weapons—clearly had an inhibiting effect on Moscow. This is evident from a speech Khrushchev gave in 1961, in which he declared:

> There was a time when American Secretary of State Dulles brandished thermonuclear bombs and followed a policy from "positions of strength" with regard to the socialist countries. He followed this policy with regard to all states which disagreed with the imperialist claims of the United States. That was barefaced atomic blackmail, but it had to be reckoned with at the time because we did not possess sufficient means of retaliation; and if we did, they were not as many and not of the same power as those of our opponents.

Dulles also never lost sight of his political aims in considering arms control plans. A major Dulles concern was the cohesion of the Atlantic Alliance, which meant close ties to West Germany and to his friend Adenauer.

After Stassen's fall, one of his assistants, Robert E. Matteson, delivered a speech in which, without naming names but in terms apparent to all, he discussed the rival Dulles and Stassen schools of thought. He stated that the group with Stassen's viewpoint favored a policy of relaxation of tension, which he described as "one which would recognize the strength of the Soviet bloc and would do more to encourage the liberating tendencies within the bloc. It would accept the Soviet Union as an equal power and would encourage the gradual evolution of the Soviet system toward freedom." By contrast, the other group favored an "increased tension policy," one "which would emphasize more the weakness of the Soviet bloc, would look toward pressuring the Soviet leadership into agreements which represent concessions by the Soviets to their own interest, and would look toward striving to pressure the Soviet system into a collapse without a war."

The Dulles-Adenauer relationship was a pillar of that pressure-the-Russians approach. Eisenhower was whipsawed by the two lines of argument and came down on Dulles's side in the end. Yet Stassen's hard work and imaginative thinking had a logical appeal and, in the longer view, helped prepare the way psychologically for subsequent Soviet-American relationships.

The London Conference, whatever its prospects may have been, was effectively killed in the summer of 1957 with a demonstration that the balance of power was shifting and that the deficiency in Soviet weaponry (to which Khrushchev would allude in 1961) was coming to an end. What occurred was the introduction of a new weapons system.

The Soviet Union on August 26, 1957, announced the first test of an intercontinental ballistic missile (ICBM). Six weeks later, on October 4, came the first *Sputnik*. These two events shook American confidence in its military and scientific superiority and opened for the Russians an opportunity, eagerly seized by Khrushchev, to engage in rocket-rattling nuclear diplomacy, which at times amounted to nuclear blackmail. Less than a year earlier, at the height of the Suez crisis, the Russians had threatened to hurl nuclear rockets at Great Britain, which, with France, had invaded Egypt. The threat added to world alarm at the time, even though it was viewed in Washington as merely a form of political blackmail.

President Eisenhower, in the wake of what he later described as "the current wave of near-hysteria" induced by *Sputnik* and the ICBM, created the Gaither Committee, a group of eminent Americans headed by H. Rowan Gaither, Jr., then board chairman of the Ford Foundation. The Committee, originally formed to examine chiefly the need for an American bomb shelter program, broadened its scope, and its findings, part of which became known at the time, pictured a rapidly arming Soviet Union with a capability by late 1959 of launching 100 ICBM's against the United States. In reality, as later intelligence showed, the Russians did not have sufficient ICBM's to represent what the United States considered a serious threat until 1962.

But the psychological damage had been done, and Khrushchev exploited it to the fullest. In the United States, such projections of Soviet strength formed the basis of the "missile gap" charge that Senator John F. Kennedy used in his 1960 Presidential campaign against Richard Nixon, Eisenhower's Vice-President.

But before Khrushchev began to exploit the Soviet ICBM, and before the Democrats exploited the alleged missile gap, there was a major, secret development in the action-reaction phenomenon in the arms race.

In November, 1954, Eisenhower had been presented with a proposal to build, at a cost of about $35 million, thirty high-altitude reconnaissance planes of the type that came to be known as the U-2. Design and development were already well under way, and the President had approved production plans. Eisenhower later justified this move on the grounds that "our relative position in intelligence, compared to that of the Soviets, could scarcely have been worse." About that, there is today no quarrel.

The plane was test-flown over the United States to determine the ability of its cameras and to see whether, flying at 70,000 feet or more above the earth, it could be picked up and tracked by American radar. Its distance-shrinking cameras produced incredibly detailed photographs from fourteen miles up, and its tracking by ground radar proved imperfect. Furthermore, fighter planes at that time could not operate at higher than 50,000 feet. The risk of flying the U-2 over the Soviet Union seemed clearly outweighed by the potential gains.

When Eisenhower returned from the Geneva summit meeting after the rejection of his Open Skies proposal, he directed that the U-2 should overfly Russia. After two flights from Weisbaden, in West Germany, the U-2, in the summer of 1956, flew its first mission over the Soviet Union. It covered both Moscow and Leningrad.

The U-2 was a well-kept secret. Its limitation was the requirement for cloudless skies between the plane and the ground, a relatively rare event in much of the Soviet Union, but the pictures it brought back were a giant step forward in American intelligence gathering. The data it gathered, however, came too late to counter the false assumptions that went into the Gaither Committee predictions.

Once the Soviet ICBM program began, the U-2 became an even more essential tool for U.S. intelligence. U-2 photographs disclosed that *Sputnik* had been launched from the Tyuratam Missile Range. The Semipalatinsk nuclear test site was identified by U-2 photographs, as was a missile air defense development site. Before the flights were discontinued in 1960, U-2's had flown between twenty and thirty times over the Soviet Union, including runs over the Kamchatka Peninsula on the Pacific Ocean.

Thomas S. Gates, Jr., Eisenhower's last Secretary of Defense, told the Senate Foreign Relations Committee that information had been obtained "on airfields, aircraft, missiles, missile testing and training, special weapons storage, submarine production, atomic production and aircraft deployment . . . all types of vital information." Allen Dulles, then head of the Central Intelligence Agency, which directed the U-2 flights, said in 1968 that the planes were "primarily for the purpose of keeping the West advised of the new Soviet battle order of its guided missiles." Such data, of course, were vital in the arms control field.

Although this intelligence strongly affected American thinking about arms control proposals, the public knew nothing of the U-2 and its photographs until 1960. What was known, and what had a far more immediate effect on the public during the Eisenhower years, was the danger of radioactive fallout from nuclear tests.

The bombs that fell on Hiroshima and Nagasaki had been detonated well above the ground, and there had been no reports of fallout and its resulting damage to humans until long afterward. A dramatic example of the dangers, however, came on March 1, 1954, at a tiny atoll in the Pacific called Bikini, where the United States was testing a hydrogen weapon. From the mushroom cloud that billowed upward for more than 100,000 feet, the heavier particles of debris fell, not to the west, as had been anticipated, but to the east. Within an hour, as Ralph Lapp and Jack Schubert recounted in their book *Radiation*, "a soft rain of whitish ash was falling fifty miles downwind. Several hours later the ashy rain began to fall a hundred miles from the bomb site."

Those most seriously radiated by the fallout were twenty-three Japanese fishermen on a tuna trawler, the ironically named *Lucky Dragon*. After the ship reached Japan and scientists discovered what had occurred, there was an international uproar. Not until February 15, 1955, did the U.S. Atomic Energy Commission report that about 7,000 square miles of territory downwind from the blast "was so contaminated that survival might have depended upon prompt evacuation of the area or upon taking shelter or other protective measures."

American testing in the atmosphere, and Soviet testing as well, continued, but public pressure to do something about the fallout menace mounted rapidly. In the 1956 Presidential campaign, Democratic candidate Adlai Stevenson called for a ban on nuclear tests, although it was not clear whether he meant all tests or was merely calling for a unilateral American halt to testing. The proposal further inflamed passions over the issue. Eisenhower, though it was then evident he would easily be re-elected, found himself on the defensive. His Administration was attacked for seeming to claim, as its enemies declared, that "radiation is good for you." There is evidence that, prior to the Stevenson proposal, the President had nearly agreed to Stassen's suggestion to untie a test ban proposal from the larger package of American arms control measures, but the political move by Stevenson killed the idea.

By October, 1957, Japanese Prime Minister Nobusuke Kishi was writing the President about "the urgent necessity of ending all nuclear test explosions." Eisenhower, disturbed by the public outcry, told Stassen to work up a proposal for a one- or two-year test ban, during which an inspection system within the Soviet Union and the United States could be installed.

But by the time the London Conference ended a few months later, the President, at Dulles's urging, had reverted to drawing tight again the knot that bound the test ban proposal to other arms control measures. Eisenhower was now arguing that if a test ban were "to alleviate rather than merely to conceal the threat of nuclear war" it "should be undertaken as a part of a meaningful program to reduce that threat."

It was an untenable position. By 1958, with continuing American and Soviet tests further polluting the world's atmosphere, immense pressure had built up in the United States and elsewhere outside the Communist bloc for a test ban agreement separate from all other issues. Dulles, fearing that he could not withstand such pressure, seized upon proposals for convening a conference of technical experts on the practical problem of supervision and control of a test ban, an idea suggested to Khrushchev by the President on April 28, 1958. To Washington's surprise, Khrushchev, eleven days later, accepted. Dulles himself conceded that he had "broken the package."

To head the American delegation to the eight-nation Conference on the Discontinuance of Nuclear Weapons Tests, Eisenhower named James Brown Fisk, executive vice-president of Bell Telephone Laboratories and a member of the President's Scientific Advisory Committee. Dr. Fisk was assisted by Ernest O. Lawrence, a senior nuclear scientist, who had headed the University of California's radiation laboratory, and Robert F. Backer, a former Atomic Energy Commission member. A similar gathering, a ten-nation "Conference of Experts for the Study of Possible Means Which Might be Helpful in Preventing Surprise Attack," was also agreed to by Moscow and Washington. William C. Foster, a Republican businessman and Pentagon official, who later headed the Arms Control and Disarmament Agency, led the American delegation to the ten-nation conference. He had also served on the Gaither Committee.

The test ban meeting produced a Soviet-American agreement, backed by the six other participating nations, for a worldwide network of land- and ship-based control posts. A degree of on-site inspection on the territory of the two superpowers was also agreed on. The ten-nation meeting on surprise attack, however, ended in an impasse over how to separate political from technical issues; nevertheless, it forced both sides to come to grips with a number of arms control problems.

The test ban experts, Soviet and American, came up with a plan for locating control posts with respect to earthquake areas of the world. The proposed network included 24 posts in North America, 6 in Europe, 37 in Asia, 7 in Australia, 16 in South America, 16 in Africa, 4 in Antarctica, and 60 control posts on islands and "about 10 ships." The actual number of posts, according to the report, could "be determined only in the process of actually disposing them around the globe."

The Soviet willingness to agree surprised—indeed dumbfounded—Washington. Further efforts at negotiations took place in Geneva with the United States, the Soviet Union, and Great Britain, then the world's three nuclear powers, participating. Overriding the doubters in his Administration, Eisenhower offered a year's suspension of tests during the talks. The offer was not totally gratuitous. Eisenhower later recounted that the risks of such an offer were reduced, because the suspension would not begin "until after the completion of our Hardtack series of tests in the Pacific" and because the offer was conditioned on Soviet agreement for a similar test moratorium.

The Russians agreed to the temporary ban during the talks. It was to take effect on October 31, 1958. However, the Soviet Union conducted tests on both November 1 and 3, past the unofficial cutoff date, as the Atomic Energy Commission's monitoring system discovered. Eisenhower did not revoke the American moratorium but he did announce on November 7 that the Soviet testing had relieved the United States of its obligation. However, he agreed to stick to the moratorium and, since there were no further Soviet tests, the series apparently being completed, the ban continued.

But while the Geneva talks were trying to turn the experts' views into an agreement, results of the Hardtack series of American tests were presented. The tests demonstrated that nuclear explosions could be shielded in underground caverns in such a way that they would not register on the proposed seismic detection system. Thus, it was argued, the agreement with the Soviet Union had been based on incomplete data, since large sized nuclear tests could be conducted clandestinely. The American findings were made known at Geneva, but the Russians refused to consider them.

This development put the United States in a very difficult position before the world, especially since it was well known that there was dissent in and out of the government over a test ban on any terms. The President finally suggested a ban on atmospheric tests only, permitting the difficult-to-check underground tests by both sides to continue. This was the formula finally agreed on during the Kennedy Administration, but the time was not yet right, and Khrushchev rejected the plan.

A second attempt by the experts failed, and Eisenhower announced that the American test moratorium would end on December 31, 1959, although the United States would not resume tests without prior public announcement. There now ensued fruitless efforts to agree on a "threshold" for underground tests, that is, the seismic magnitude above which tests would be prohibited.

Khrushchev, in rejecting the limited test ban proposal, suggested that the two sides try harder to agree on the number of annual trips of inspection teams that would be needed to check suspicious events on the territory of the two superpowers and their allies. In the course of lengthy talks, the United States slowly whittled down the number of inspections per year to twenty, eventually to eight, and hinted at less.

The kind of problem inherent in Soviet-American arms negotiations is illustrated by an incident that occurred in 1962, when the number of such on-site inspections was being argued. Khrushchev apparently concluded that the United States would agree to three. He contended that such an arrangement had been indicated to him by Arthur Dean, a law partner of Dulles and sometime arms control negotiator. Dean denied giving any such indication. The American Government had believed that, if Khrushchev raised the number of annual inspection trips to three, a compromise could then be sought between his three and the American offer of eight. Khrushchev declared that he had been double-crossed, despite American disclaimers, and the episode left bad feelings all around.

In Washington, the military largely opposed a total test ban on the grounds of necessary weapons development. Others contended that scientists would leave their laboratories if barred from experimenting, whereas Russian scientists could be forced to continue work, thus giving the Soviet Union a jump on the United States against the day when tests might be ordered again.

The test ban by now was a national issue, to be debated in the Congress. There Senator Hubert H. Humphrey, head of a disarmament subcommittee, was the leading advocate. He was aided by Senator Clinton P. Anderson, the New Mexico Democrat who had served variously as chairman and vice-chairman of the Joint Committee on Atomic Energy.

American scientists entered the political fray with a vengeance.

They were divided vehemently on the issue. Some lined up on the negative side, behind Edward Teller, widely touted as the "father of the H-bomb," while others backed the equally prestigious Hans Bethe on the positive side. British Prime Minister Harold Macmillan flew to Moscow and to Washington, trying to arrange a compromise on the on-site inspection issue. Meanwhile, France became the fourth member of the nuclear club by exploding its first bomb in the atmosphere over Algeria on February 13, 1959.

Whatever possibility of agreement existed was ended with a shattering blow that occurred in the skies over the Soviet Union on May 1, 1960, when Francis Gary Powers's U-2 was shot down by a Soviet missile near Sverdlovsk, deep in the Soviet Union. A new summit conference was about to begin in Paris. The test ban was to have been a major topic. Khrushchev was caught in a serious internal Kremlin political situation because he had been looking with favor on Eisenhower, who now reluctantly admitted ordering the U-2 flights, as a "man of peace." In Paris, Khrushchev demanded an apology he surely knew the President could not and would not give. He revoked the invitation for Eisenhower to visit the Soviet Union and announced that he would have nothing more to do with the President. Arms control and all other East-West issues were shelved, and further discussion awaited the election and inauguration of a new American President.

Eisenhower wanted to end the test moratorium but decided to leave that decision to his successor. When John F. Kennedy became President-elect, Eisenhower privately emphasized to him that "our nation should resume needed tests without delay."

In this final period of the Eisenhower Administration there was one accomplishment—the Antarctic Treaty, signed in Washington on December 1, 1959, by the United States, the Soviet Union, Great Britain, France, Japan, South Africa, New Zealand, Australia, Argentina, Chile, Belgium, and Norway. The treaty, approved by the U.S. Senate on August 10, 1960, a few months after the U-2 incident, by a vote of 66 to 21, provided for maintaining the region around the South Pole as a nuclear-free zone, subject to inspection without a veto. Subsequent inspections were made by American officials, but not by those of the Soviet Union.

Far more important, however, was an incident that occurred in Paris when the four leaders Eisenhower, Khrushchev, Macmillan, and French President Charles de Gaulle had their only meeting before the summit conference was aborted.

At this meeting, Eisenhower defended the U-2 flights against Khrushchev's charge of espionage. De Gaulle noted that in the past few days a Soviet satellite had been passing over France and, for all he knew, might be taking reconnaissance photographs. Eisenhower recounted in his memoirs what then transpired: "Khrushchev broke in to say he was talking about airplanes, not about satellites. He said any nation in the world who wanted to photograph the Soviet areas by satellites was completely free to do so."

It was a startling statement, with momentous implications for the future.

III. First Limited Agreements

Some say that it is useless to speak of world peace . . . until the leaders of the Soviet Union adopt a more enlightened attitude. I hope they do so. I believe we can help them do it. But I also believe that we must re-examine our own attitude as individuals and as a nation, for our attitude is as essential as theirs. . . . Our problems are man-made; therefore they can be solved by man.

President JOHN F. KENNEDY
June 10, 1963

The faces around the National Security Council table, at 10 A.M. on August 31, 1961, were expressive of gloom, and with every reason. The day before, the Soviet Union had announced that it was resuming nuclear testing in the atmosphere. An intimation of the news had been picked up by American monitors, who had intercepted a message two hours before the formal announcement, and President Kennedy had called his top advisers together to decide what the United States should do.

Kennedy's New Frontier, so full of hope and glowing words, had gotten off to a shattering start. First there had been the disastrous Bay of Pigs incident. Then Khrushchev, quite likely because he had interpreted the young President's handling of that abortive effort to overthrow Cuba's Fidel Castro as a sign of weakness, had heated up the Berlin issue. And less than three weeks before the Soviet resumption of testing, the Berlin Wall had gone up, while the United States stood by helplessly. Now, a critical arms control issue had been added to the President's problems.

Kennedy had long been interested in arms control. He had come to office determined to do what he believed Eisenhower had not done—press hard for meaningful agreements. The first statement at his first press conference, on January 25, 1961, was the inevitable announcement that the new Administration would review the test ban situation. Kennedy had named John J. McCloy coordinator of disarmament activities. McCloy, a senior states-man, former High Commissioner in Germany, a member of the Establishment, and a Republican, was the ideal appointee for a new President who had won a narrow election. McCloy had been an Eisenhower arms control adviser, well-known for his cautious views. His selection at the outset of the Kennedy Administration thus mollified those who feared that the new President might take risks in regard to national security. (McCloy remains active as head of President Nixon's advisory group to the Arms Control and Disarmament Agency.)

During his campaign for the Presidency, Kennedy had com-plained that fewer than one hundred men scattered through the government had anything to do with arms control and disarma-ment, a theme that engendered considerable public response. Partly in reaction to Kennedy's charges, President Eisenhower, in the fall of the election year, had created the Disarmament Administration within the Department of State. After his inau-guration, Kennedy asked Congress to establish a new agency to deal with all arms control matters, but not until September, 1961, did Congress create the Arms Control and Disarmament Agency (ACDA). Theodore C. Sorensen, in his book *Kennedy*, described the President as interested primarily in influencing world opinion on the disarmament issue, but Sorensen added that Kennedy in time "underwent a degree of redemption on this subject" by coming to believe that arms control measures really might be achieved, thus releasing funds for domestic programs. The new agency's very name was indicative of congressional doubts. The ACDA represented a compromise on the part of those who hoped for the utopia of total disarmament and those who felt it more realistic to attempt to control the arms race. The ACDA absorbed the small group already at work in the State Department.

For the first time since Stassen's loss of influence in 1957, the United States gathered together a full staff of arms control experts. McCloy, whose report to Kennedy was the basis for establishing the ACDA, bowed out (but still served in an advisory capacity), and William C. Foster became the agency's first head. Adrian S. Fisher, a lawyer who had worked for both the Atomic Energy Commission and the State Department, was the able backstop, serving into the early months of the Nixon Administration.

But events did not wait for orderly development of new policies by the new Administration. On Inauguration Day, Khrushchev, who had totally severed relations with Eisenhower, cabled the new President his hopes for a "radical improvement" in Soviet-American relations. As a gesture to Kennedy, Khrushchev freed the two surviving crewmen of a U.S. Air Force RB-47 electronic snooping plane that had been shot down just north of the Soviet Union over the Barents Sea the previous July 1. Khrushchev's act, said Kennedy, removed "a serious obstacle to improvement of Soviet-American relations."

This gesture, however, had not been unexpected. Between election and inauguration, two men who became key members of Kennedy's Administration, Jerome B. Wiesner and Walt W. Rostow, had met in Moscow with Soviet officials. The occasion was one of the Pugwash conferences, named after the Nova Scotia home of Cleveland financier Cyrus Eaton, who had initiated the series of meetings that continue to this day, in the belief that unofficial East-West gatherings would help Moscow and Washington better understand each other.

Wiesner, a nuclear expert who became Kennedy's White House science adviser, was the leading advocate of arms control throughout the early 1960's. He wielded considerable influence because of his ability to grasp and evaluate facts quickly. Wiesner was perhaps the first person in a high position to sense the action-reaction phenomenon. He had been a principal backer of the Stevenson test ban proposal in 1958 and now sought to make Kennedy see the problem from the Soviet point of view. In 1958, Wiesner had been a staff expert at the surprise attack conference in the delegation led by William Foster. Rostow, an economic historian, who later became President Johnson's assistant for national security affairs and a leading advocate of the Vietnam War, was equally anxious to get the Kennedy Administration off to a good start in its relations with the Soviet Union. But he was less of an optimist than Wiesner.

The Wiesner-Rostow team, under cover of the Pugwash meeting in Moscow, urged Soviet officials to release the RB-47 fliers as an opening gesture of goodwill. Arthur M. Schlesinger's *A Thousand Days: John F. Kennedy in the White House* related that, in the course of the talks, V. V. Kuznetsov of the Soviet Foreign Office mentioned Kennedy's missile-gap campaign charges, adding that a massive American buildup would necessarily bring a Soviet reaction. Rostow countered that the purpose of any Kennedy armament program would only be to maintain the stability of the American deterrent.

In February, the new Defense Secretary, Robert S. McNamara, revealed to newsmen that after examination of the facts, he had found the missile gap to be nonexistent—as Eisenhower, to no avail, had indignantly contended all along. Nonetheless, debate over the issue persisted in the United States into late 1961. The Air Force, according to Schlesinger, contended that the Russians had 600 to 800 ballistic missiles; the Central Intelligence Agency (CIA) estimated they had 450; the Navy's estimate was only 200. The figures were not broken down as between intercontinental missiles (ICBM's) and medium-range missiles (MRBM's).

(It is now known that the Soviet Union had concentrated first on building a medium-range missile force, targeted on Western Europe.) After he pulled Soviet missiles out of Cuba in 1962, Khrushchev, on January 19, 1963, gave the only specific figures ever released of the Soviet long-range force. He said that at that time the United States was still covered by 80 to 120 missiles. If correct, all the estimates given Kennedy as late as the fall of 1961 were far too high.

But the action-reaction cycle induced by the Soviet ICBM and *Sputnik* in 1957 was still in motion, and Kennedy did nothing to halt it. A nuclear-powered submarine system with nuclear-tipped Polaris missiles that could be fired from under water had been given a go-ahead by Eisenhower in the wake of the Gaither Committee's alarming predictions. A land-based ICBM program of Minuteman missiles also was accelerated after *Sputnik*, and Kennedy approved what eventually became a force of 1,054 missiles deep in concrete silos.

The result of these programs, despite all the talk in the early Kennedy years of nuclear "overkill," was to widen the missile gap in favor of the United States. One reason for Kennedy's acquiescence, according to Schlesinger, was that the President "went along with the policy of multiplying Polaris and Minuteman . . . missiles" as a concession to the Pentagon because he had already rejected the Air Force demand for the high-altitude B-70 bomber. Some observers have speculated that, after the Bay of Pigs debacle, Kennedy felt he had to show strength and thus could not afford to oppose the development of additional missiles. Foster sought in mid-1961 to win the President's approval for a proposal to Moscow calling for a mutual percentage of cuts in missiles, bombers, and naval vessels, but Kennedy replied that it was much too soon for such a move. Six years later, McNamara said that the 1961 buildup of the two missile systems "was necessitated by a lack of accurate information," and he acknowledged that "clearly the Soviet buildup" after the 1964 ouster of Khrushchev was "in part a reaction to our own buildup since the beginning of this decade."

Thus, although Kennedy came to office determined to control and slow the arms race, he actually fueled it with the rapid buildup of new weapons systems. But the atmosphere of the early Kennedy years was not one to suggest a cutback in strategic weapons. Furthermore, a meeting in June, 1961, with Khrushchev in Vienna raised alarms about a new Soviet-American confrontation over Berlin and confirmed the view of the fearful that a fuller complement of missiles was essential.

At the Vienna meeting, Khrushchev and Kennedy talked fruitlessly about a test ban treaty, which was once again being negotiated at Geneva. Khrushchev declared that more than three on-site inspections would constitute espionage. More important, however, he grimly put pressure on Kennedy over Berlin. According to Sorenson, the President believed if the Soviet leader "had meant what he said about Berlin, the prospects for nuclear war were now very real—for Kennedy had meant what he said" in declaring the United States would honor its commitment to the freedom of West Berlin.

Kennedy returned to Washington to raise a public alarm and strengthen the American military establishment in preparation for a showdown over Berlin. There is little doubt now that he overreacted.

It is against this background that the National Security Council meeting of August 31, 1961, began.

By the day of the meeting, the Berlin crisis had reached such proportions that Kennedy had sent an armored column from West Germany into West Berlin to show U.S. determination to protect the city. Vice-President Lydon B. Johnson had flown to West Berlin to declare to the alarmed citizens of the beleaguered city that the United States pledged "our lives, our fortunes and our sacred honor" in support of their cause. In 1962, Khrushchev contended that the Soviet Union had been negotiating a test ban in good faith "until the President of the United States announced a mobilization of the armed forces and started threatening us with war."

The Soviet announcement of new tests was accompanied by charges that the United States was "fanning up the arms race" and justifications that "the Soviet Union considers it its duty to take all necessary measures" to ensure its security. At the National Security Council meeting, some council members advised the President to resume American tests at once, but Kennedy demurred. He knew there would be a worldwide reaction against the Russians and he followed Vice-President Johnson's advice to "let Khrushchev take the heat for a little while."

Kennedy later announced a renewal of underground tests to begin after September 5, 1961, but not until the following April 15 did he order renewed atmospheric testing. In part, the delay was to gain maximum propaganda advantage; but in part, it was due to American unpreparedness for a new test series. The United States had been caught napping.

Soviet resumption of testing, although it hit the public with force, had been preceded by considerable evidence that such a move was coming. During a July 27, 1961, meeting in the Soviet Crimean city of Sochi, Khrushchev told McCloy that he was being pressured to resume tests by his scientists and military leaders. He also dropped a hint of an incredible 100-megaton bomb, and when the tests did resume, two days after the Soviet announcement, the explosions reached the 60 megaton range, far beyond anything tested before or since by the United States.

American officials did their best to deprecate the magnitude of the Soviet tests, although it was believed that the Kremlin was somehow trying to alter the balance of power, since the balance at the moment still was very much in the United States' favor.

Erection of the Berlin Wall actually ended the Berlin crisis by blocking the hemorrhage of East Germans into the West, but it was not evident at the time and the crisis did not end until Khrushchev publicly lifted the deadline he had proclaimed for signing a German peace treaty with the Communist East Germans. Had the Soviet Union held to the deadline, the United States would have been in the position of having to fire the first shot if it had refused to honor East German control of the routes into West Berlin.

Far more serious than the Berlin crisis was Khrushchev's bold attempt in 1962 to overcome American nuclear superiority by secretly emplacing missiles in Cuba. It was estimated then that the Soviet Union had only 75 ICBM's; the United States had 156 ICBM's ready to fire at the time of the October Cuban crisis, plus 144 missiles aboard nine Polaris submarines. Thomas W. Wolfe analyzed the reasoning behind the Soviet move in his book *Soviet Power and Europe: the Evolution of a Political-Military Posture, 1945–64:*

> The decision to deploy a force of Soviet-manned missiles to Cuba, evidently taken sometime in the spring of 1962, appears to have resulted mainly from the cumulative frustrations of policy setbacks suffered by Khrushchev during the previous three or four years. They included not only the failure of Soviet pressure tactics to obtain concessions from the West on such specific pivotal issues as Berlin, but also the deflation of Khrushchev's hopes that a diplomacy backed by the exploits of Soviet missile and space technology would weaken the resolution of the Western alliance and erode its confidence in the protective commitments of the United States. On the contrary, Khrushchev found that, by early 1962, the parallel collapse of his Berlin offensive and of the "missile gap" myth was serving to reinforce the assurances of American officials that the West still enjoyed an ample margin of strategic superiority. Moreover, he was now in the increasingly uncomfortable position some of his own military men had feared: namely, that he had been overambitious in trying to gain more political mileage from Soviet missiles than the actual strategic balance warranted. Beyond this, of course, Khrushchev was confronted in early 1962 by growing criticism of his strategic leadership from the Chinese wing of the world Communist movement, and in Cuba, itself, Castro was pressing for some form of tangible Soviet commitment to the defense of the first Communist regime to be established in the Western Hemisphere.

Emplacement of some forty medium-range Soviet missiles in Cuba, in a single stroke, would have seriously reduced the Soviet Union's missile gap, since warning time in the United States for a missile fired from Cuba would have been almost nil. It is generally believed that Khrushchev intended, once the missiles were in place, to use them as a bargaining point in reopening the Berlin issue in the fall of 1962.

In the Cuban crisis, the United States had overwhelming conventional military superiority because of its closeness to the island, and because the Soviet Union, which lacked a comparable naval force, was so far away. In his October 22 speech to the nation revealing the crisis, the President threatened the Soviet Union with a nuclear holocaust if the Kremlin should fire a nuclear missile from Cuba. The effect of this move can still only be guessed. Kennedy said bluntly, "It shall be the policy of this nation to regard any nuclear missile launched from Cuba against any nation in the Western Hemisphere as an attack by the Soviet Union on the United States, requiring a full retaliatory response upon the Soviet Union." Thus, Kennedy put the onus of starting a nuclear war on Khrushchev. Furthermore, there is reason to believe that the worldwide alert of all American forces, both conventional and nuclear, brought home to the Kremlin leaders the real possibility of a massive strike at their nation if the missiles were not pulled out of Cuba as Kennedy demanded.

Kennedy told the nation, and the world, "We are in as grave a crisis as mankind has been in," and, for thirteen days, the whole world seemed to hold its breath. In the end, Khrushchev retreated and withdrew the missiles. Although Kennedy carefully refrained from public boasting, it was evident to all which side had backed down.

In August, before the crisis, test ban and nonproliferation treaty talks were going on between the two superpowers. Much later, it was reported that on August 25 Moscow had told Peking that it intended to reject the latest American proposal for a partial test ban. But after the crisis, the Kremlin's attitude took a new turn. Berlin was forgotten, and peaceful coexistence with the United States was once again the theme.

In this post-crisis atmosphere, Khrushchev indicated renewed interest in a nuclear test ban treaty. For reasons of his own, he chose negotiating with the United States rather than embarking on a new nuclear arms program. He exchanged letters with Kennedy on the issue, but the two leaders were unable to break the old impasse over on-site inspection. The United States cut the number of inspections it demanded to seven—with conditions—while Khrushchev vacillated from three to two to none and back to three—also with conditions. He was evidently under pressure and getting contradictory advice from his own domestic critics, who may have been emboldened by his Cuban fiasco.

On March 21, 1963, Kennedy told newsmen that the reason he was trying so hard for a test ban was because

> personally I am haunted by the feeling that by 1970, unless we are successful, there may be ten nuclear powers instead of four and by 1975, fifteen or twenty. . . . I see the possibility of the President of the United States having to face a world in which fifteen or twenty or twenty-five nations may have these weapons. I regard that as the greatest possible danger and hazard.

By May, he was even more pessimistic when he commented at a press conference that, if there were no treaty, "perhaps the genie is out of the bottle and we'll never get him back in again."

Kennedy decided, as Schlesinger put it, that the time had come for a major address on peace, in a fresh context, to save the "dying negotiations" with the Soviet Union. He chose to do so in a commencement speech at American University on June 10, seizing on what Schlesinger described as an ungracious and sulky letter from Khrushchev in which he had agreed to a Presidential suggestion for sending a special emissary to Moscow to try to break the test ban impasse.

The Kennedy speech provided an opening for Khrushchev. The President, speaking of "the most important topic on earth:

world peace" said he did not mean a "Pax Americana." He spoke sympathetically of the huge Soviet losses in World War II, and he called on Americans to re-examine their own attitudes toward the Cold War. "We are both caught up," he said, "in a vicious and dangerous cycle in which suspicion on one side breeds suspicion on the other, and new weapons beget counterweapons."

Kennedy announced that discussions would soon begin in Moscow "looking toward early agreement on a comprehensive test ban treaty." The response came quickly. Kennedy's speech was published in the Soviet press, and soon thereafter almost fifteen years of continuous jamming of Voice of America broadcasts ended. Of more importance, during a speech in East Berlin on July 2, Khrushchev accepted what he had long rejected: a treaty banning tests in the atmosphere and in outer space but permitting underground tests, thus avoiding the inspection nettle.

Once this Kremlin policy was settled, it took only a few weeks to negotiate the remaining details so long under discussion among the United States, Great Britain, and the Soviet Union. Kennedy sent W. Averell Harriman, an old Moscow hand, to the Soviet capital as head of the American delegation, and the President personally quarterbacked every move in the negotiations from the White House. The President was determined, once a treaty was in sight, that "no quibbling over language or sniping from his subordinates would prevent it."

Kennedy hoped that Moscow could persuade China to sign such a treaty, but by then the Moscow-Peking quarrel had become far more serious than was realized in the West. Kennedy also offered American aid to France for underground testing in an equally vain effort to win the assent of President de Gaulle.

The treaty was initialed in Moscow on July 25, 1963, after ten days of intensive negotiations. To win Senate approval, Kennedy rallied public opinion through television and press conferences and made personal contact with potential senatorial opponents. The core of the Kennedy argument was that while there are "risks inherent in any treaty, the far greater risks to our security

"Let's Get A Lock For This Thing"

—from *Straight Herblock* (Simon & Schuster, 1964)

are the risks of unrestricted testing." Some opponents were won over by promises of standby readiness to resume atmospheric testing, as proposed by Democratic Senator Henry M. Jackson, who has reviewed such preparations annually ever since. The intention was that the United States would not again be caught unprepared should the Soviet Union resume testing despite the treaty.

The American public accepted Kennedy's reasoning, as did most of the Senate, which consented to the treaty on September 24 by a vote of 80 to 19, far more than the necessary two-thirds. Thus culminated long arguments and lengthy negotiations over a test ban, a plan first suggested in the United States by Vannevar Bush in 1952 as a technique to prevent the two superpowers from testing H-bombs.

Although there were many contributing factors that led to agreement on the test ban, the treaty demonstrated that there could be exceptions to a maxim once advanced by Lawrence D. Weiler, an American arms control expert who is currently counselor to the director of the Arms Control and Disarmament Agency. The Weiler maxim declared that "the trouble is not that the Soviets and Americans do not have the same positions; the trouble is that they do not have them at the same time."

Before their interests finally coincided to produce agreement, both Moscow and Washington switched positions on formulations and details. These changes generally reflected a new reading of the balance of power and of the national interest involved, or thought to be involved.

In the United States, most of the discussions, pro and con, save some dependent on secret intelligence, were carried on in the open. In the Soviet Union, it is now quite clear, a factor not even mentioned at the bargaining table was involved—Moscow's deteriorating relations with Peking.

When Harriman arrived in Moscow for the final negotiations, there was a sign of this split. A Chinese delegation headed by Teng Hsiao-ping, secretary-general of the Communist Party, had come in what is now regarded as a last effort to resolve the growing Sino-Soviet quarrel and was ostentatiously snubbed. Khrushchev openly turned from his business with the Chinese delegates in order to meet with Harriman.

When the treaty was opened for the signatures of other countries, Khrushchev called for every nation's adherence, knowing the Chinese would not sign. He especially sought signatures of as many of the Communist nations as possible. Only a handful of small nations then politically close to China refused to join in the treaty.

China, as expected, refused to sign on the grounds that the test ban treaty was a form of Soviet-American collusion designed to prevent China from becoming an equal superpower. De Gaulle's France also refused to join, claiming that the test ban did not reduce armaments but only sought to protect the privileged position of the two superpowers. In all, 101 nations eventually signed. The treaty has had two major effects: it has ended, except for the occasional French and Chinese atmospheric tests, the nuclear contamination of the earth, which alarmed so many who were fearful of the consequences of nuclear fallout, and it has been a step toward curbing the ability of nonnuclear nations to enter the nuclear club, since testing is essential to creating a nuclear arsenal.

In the early years of Soviet-Chinese friendship, the Peking Government had closely followed the Moscow line on disarmament issues. In 1958, Peking called for an Asian nuclear-free zone, as did Khrushchev. But by 1960, the Sino-Soviet rift led China to declare that "any international agreement concerning disarmament, without the formal participation of the People's Republic of China and the signature of its delegate, cannot, of course, have any binding force on her." In 1957, after the launching of *Sputnik* and the widespread belief it induced that the United States had lost its pre-eminent position, Mao Tse-tung had gone to Moscow. There he declared that "the East wind" was now "prevailing over the West wind" and that therefore the Soviet Union should use its new power, in the form of nuclear blackmail if not outright force, to demand concessions from the United States. On October 15, 1957, according to what the Chinese said in 1963, the Soviet Union concluded with China an "agreement of new technology for national defense," an agreement Moscow "unilaterally tore up" on June 20, 1959. The 1963 account of this affair added that Moscow "refused to provide China with a sample of an atomic bomb and technical data concerning its manufacture."

Whether there was a firm Soviet promise to provide a sample bomb to the Chinese remains unclear. What is clear is that Moscow halted aid in all forms to Peking. In 1960, Krushchev suddenly withdrew all Soviet experts from China. Peking bitterly complained that Khrushchev had canceled the agreements "as a gift" to Eisenhower during his visit to the United States. Eisenhower later recounted that Khrushchev did bring up the subject of China, but that the conversation was both limited and inconclusive. Khrushchev's failure in the 1962 Cuban crisis brought scorn from Peking. The breach proved to be irreparable although there were efforts to seek an accommodation.

In 1964, China entered the nuclear club, declaring that it would never be the first to use nuclear weapons, a healthy position for a new nuclear power, and the Chinese have repeated this pledge after each nuclear test. The United States in 1966 attempted to lure the Chinese into signing the test ban treaty, claiming that basically the treaty was merely another form of this pledge, but Peking refused to sign, calling the treaty "a criminal concoction by the two nuclear overlords . . . to consolidate their nuclear monopoly." Peking said the proposal to link the treaty with a non-first-use pledge was an American scheme to "restrict China's development of nuclear weapons while it continues to develop them in a big way."

Another consequence of the Cuban missile crisis was the establishment of the "hot line" between Washington and Moscow, on June 21, 1963. This new communications link was a teletype —not a telephone—passing through London, Helsinki, and Stockholm, with instant coding and decoding by American and Soviet equipment in each capital.

Although the hot line agreement was not, strictly speaking, an arms control measure, its subsequent employment demonstrated its usefulness in preventing war between the superpowers due to misinformation, misunderstanding of intentions, or a combination of the two. Obviously what passes over the hot line is far more important than the device itself.

After ratification of the test ban treaty, Kennedy hoped to negotiate other agreements to limit nuclear weapons. But he was not to see his plans realized. Less than two months later, he was assassinated in Dallas, Texas. The new President, Lyndon B. Johnson, continued the American search for arms control agreements with the Soviet Union, but, like Truman, Eisenhower, and Kennedy before him, he found the range of possibilities limited both by the precarious balance of power and by the effect of extraneous events.

In his first months in office, Johnson had little time for arms control problems. But, in the Communist world, two events occurred that were to make the American President's concern with disarmament inevitable: the ouster of Khrushchev on October 15, 1964, and the explosion, the next day, of the first Chinese nuclear device. The two occurrences gave the problems of arms control a new dimension.

After Johnson's election in November to a full White House term, he sought to continue the Kennedy-Khrushchev post-Cuba *détente* with the new duumvirate in the Kremlin, Leonid Brezhnev and Alexei Kosygin, head of the Russian Communist Party and of the Soviet Government, respectively. McGeorge Bundy, who first served Kennedy and then Johnson as Special Assistant for National Security Affairs, was a strong promoter of arms control, as, of course, was the Arms Control and Disarmament Agency's William C. Foster.

However, the Vietnam War increasingly preoccupied the President and made doing business with the Soviet Union more difficult, since Moscow was actively supporting North Vietnam. In 1968, after the massive intervention of American ground forces in Vietnam, Soviet Premier Alexei Kosygin, in an interview published in *Life* magazine on February 2, 1968, said that "in the light of American aggression we cannot have normal relations with the U.S. as long as it continues the war." Johnson, however, sought to demonstrate that despite the war the United States could have normal, or near-normal, relations with the Soviet Union, and this was one reason he constantly pressed for arms agreements. Of course, like his predecessors, once he was in the White House, he came to see the overriding need of preventing a nuclear holocaust, which many believed might be the result if the Vietnam War were escalated. Thus, arms control measures did have his attention.

As part of his effort to continue a dialogue with the Soviet Union, the President in 1965 and 1966 pressed for a formal treaty to prohibit the use of outer space for military purposes, a more binding document than the resolution approved on October 17, 1963, by the U.N. General Assembly. (Approval of that resolution had been made possible by President Kennedy's agreement that it need not call for an inspection system.) Negotiations for the outer space treaty were conducted at Geneva and at the United Nations in New York, and an agreement was produced on December 8, 1966. The Senate consented to the treaty on April 25, 1967, by a vote of 88 to 0.

Johnson also sought a treaty to prevent the spread of nuclear weapons beyond the nuclear club members, who now numbered five, but such an agreement was far more difficult to achieve than the essentially pre-emptive move to ban nuclear weapons from outer space, since the two superpowers alone had the ability to use space for military purposes.

Serious discussion of a nonproliferation agreement had begun as far back as 1956, but the proposal then had a lower priority than the test ban, which itself was a technique for inhibiting the spread of nuclear weapons. However, any nation, despite having signed this treaty, could produce the nuclear component and develop the engineering necessary to fabricate a bomb, as long as the weapon was not tested. One of the aims of a nonproliferation treaty was to close this loophole.

A treaty to halt proliferation had different appeals for different nations. To the United States, it was attractive as a method of holding the nuclear club to three, then to four, and finally to five members, thus preventing national control in such inflammable areas of the world as Central Europe, the Middle East, and the Indian subcontinent.

The Soviet Union's primary interest was, and remains, to keep nuclear weapons out of West German hands. In 1963, the Russians had all but flatly told the Chinese that giving Peking such weapons would make it impossible to prevent the Americans from doing the same for the Germans. It was an ex post facto rationale, however, for Khrushchev had already withdrawn the aid Moscow had been giving Peking on nuclear development. There is good reason to believe that no Kremlin decision has ever been regretted more than the decision to help China enter the nuclear club.

The strength of the Soviet determination to keep nuclear weapons out of the hands of West Germany, born of memories of Hitler and World War II, was demonstrated by Kosygin's remarks during a 1967 press conference in London. West Germany, he said, "will have to join the agreement on nonproliferation, whether it wants it or not." Then he added this grim warning: "We will not allow the FRG [Federal Republic of Germany] to have nuclear weapons and we will take all measures to prevent it getting nuclear weapons. We say it with utter resolution."

The problem of reaching agreement on a nonproliferation treaty was complicated and delayed by an American scheme known as the Multilateral Nuclear Force (MLF). This proposal, made in the final year of the Eisenhower Administration, called for a sharing operation by the Western Allies of a seaborne missile force. The idea was advanced chiefly to appease nonnuclear

West Germany, but there were so many objections to MLF that within a short time only the United States was still backing it. Much of the MLF argument revolved around whether the scheme would give the West Germans "a finger on the nuclear trigger." The United States said no; the Soviet Union, yes. Moscow had much support in the West for its position since the possibility of Germany having the power to fire nuclear weapons was as undesirable to Western Europe as it was to the Communist world.

Another difficulty in achieving a nonproliferation treaty was protection for nonnuclear nations. Some of the countries being asked to sign a pledge of nuclear abstention were adamantly opposed to such self-denial without compensating security guarantees.

The Indians suggested a joint Soviet-American pledge to protect them against possible Chinese attack. Both Washington and Moscow shied away from such a commitment, although Johnson attempted to find a formula, including a generalized U.N. pledge, to satisfy India and other nations with similar fears. The firmest guarantee the President came up with was a public statement made on October 18, 1964, two days after the first Chinese test: "The nations that do not seek nuclear weapons can be sure that, if they need our strong support against some threat of nuclear blackmail, they will have it."

The nonproliferation treaty became the central issue at the 1965 meetings of the Eighteen-Nation Disarmament Conference in Geneva. The ENDC, as it was called, initially was composed of five Western nations (including France, which refused, and still refuses, to take its seat), five Communist nations, and eight countries considered nonaligned to either bloc. (The ENDC in 1969 was expanded by two and then by eight more nations, after which it was renamed the Conference of the Committee on Disarmament, or the CCD.)

Created by the United Nations in March, 1962, the ENDC had resumed in 1965 after a lengthy break. In August, the United States brought a draft nonproliferation treaty, and the Soviet

Union offered its version in September. Although the two drafts had a number of similar clauses, the negotiations soon became snagged over Soviet insistence that the "loophole" detected by the Russians in the American draft for the MLF scheme be closed. The Chinese reacted in June, 1966, to signs that the Soviet Union and the United States were serious about the proposed treaty with an intensification of charges that the two superpowers were in collusion. Peking declared:

> The reason why the Soviet leaders were so impatient to strike a deal on the question of prevention of nuclear proliferation was a hasty attempt to maintain the hegemony of the two nuclear powers —the Soviet Union and the United States—through such a treaty so that they may collaborate in dominating the world and at the same time to create the false impression that the international situation has relaxed so as to slack and paralyze the anti-U.S. imperialism struggle of the revolutionary people of the world.

The struggle referred to was the Communist resistance to the United States in Vietnam, where President Johnson was escalating American involvement.

Despite, or perhaps (for the Russians) because of, China's position, and despite France's continued refusal to take part, the ENDC went on.

By October, 1966, when the Chinese Red Guard movement in Peking had reached a new high in anti-Soviet vitriol, the Kremlin leaders apparently decided to modify their position in order to obtain a treaty. The Russians had been charging the United States with stalling, but Soviet Foreign Minister Andrei Gromyko went to Washington and, on October 10, signaling a change in the Soviet position, publicly declared that "it looks like both countries . . . are striving to reach agreement to facilitate the conclusion of an international agreement" on nonproliferation.

Johnson, who had met with Gromyko at the White House the day before, responded publicly by calling the talks fruitful and adding that achieving the treaty was "the thing that I think we need to do most."

Then, on October 15, Brezhnev welcomed "certain headway which has lately taken place," adding that "such a treaty would serve as a definite obstacle on the road of the further growth of the danger of a nuclear war and would create a most favorable atmosphere for progress in disarmament talks."

Once again there was a conjunction of Moscow's and Washington's interests on a step to control the arms race, despite basically irreconcilable objectives in their individual foreign policies. The Kremlin leaders put aside their earlier, firmly stated position that participation in the Vietnam conflict was a barrier to negotiations with the United States. During 1966, they also agreed to a renewal of a cultural exchange pact and to resumption of talks, this time successful, on direct airline connections between the two nations. It may be that, with the growing Sino-Soviet quarrel, the Kremlin had decided to lessen tensions with the United States. Since the United States was willing, for its own reasons, to do the same, conditions were auspicious for agreement.

By then, too, the MLF scheme was actually, if not formally, dead. The United States indicated a willingness to let the project drop, provided the Soviet Union would not press to close a treaty loophole allowing for the possibility of an eventual Western European nuclear force. The risk of that eventuality, should the day ever come when Great Britain and France would surrender their national forces to a supranational body controlled by a politically unified Western Europe, must have seemed minimal to the Kremlin, as, indeed, it still does in both the East and the West.

By mid-1967, the Soviet and U.S. drafts of a treaty were brought into line except for one key article on the traditionally troublesome subject of inspection to determine compliance with the treaty's terms. Both superpowers originally had favored use of the International Atomic Energy Agency (IAEA) to inspect peaceful atomic plants and make sure that their output was not being secretly diverted to military use. A fact of nuclear life is that a reactor built to produce electricity invariably produces the stuff of which nuclear bombs are made. Indeed, this fact has led many observers to conclude that the development of the so-called peaceful atom portends disaster. Others, however, are not so gloomy.

Several of the six European nations that constitute the European Atomic Energy Agency (Euratom)—chief among them West Germany and, to a lesser degree, Italy—opposed IAEA inspection on grounds of national security and of competitive business secrets, insisting that Euratom inspection was adequate. Efforts at a compromise that permitted a period of Euratom control before an IAEA takeover encountered Soviet opposition.

At the summit conference between President Johnson and Premier Kosygin at Glassboro, New Jersey, in June, 1967, the two leaders agreed anew on the need for a nonproliferation treaty. But by then the inspection issue in Western Europe was not the only problem. Serious reservations on the part of India, Japan, Brazil, Israel, and other nations threatened to prevent signatures of important nuclear-potential nations, even if the two super-powers were to agree.

Furthermore, the 1967 Six Day War between Israel and its Arab neighbors, in which Israel determined to go it alone without overt Western aid, raised the specter of a later round in which Israel might employ nuclear weapons. There have been recurring reports, repeatedly denied, that Israel has been making its own nuclear bombs, and, if true, there is fear that the Soviet Union might then supply Egypt with such weapons, although there is no Kremlin precedent for such a move. (The missiles sent to Cuba remained under exclusive Russian control throughout.) Israel has an advanced research program in the nuclear field, but very little preliminary research has been undertaken in Egypt.

China's first hydrogen bomb test, on June 17, 1967, intensified the doubts of India and Japan about the value of a nonproliferation treaty, since no absolute American, Soviet, or Soviet-American guarantee against China seemed likely.

Yet in the face of such developments, the Soviet-American conjunction of interests produced, on January 18, 1968, a complete agreement on a nonproliferation treaty text. The Russians yielded on the IAEA-Euratom dispute in the inspection clause. In an apparent effort to force West German adherence, Moscow accepted language that would eventually lead to a melding of the two inspection systems, language that the Bonn Government had already approved. A limit of twenty-five years on the treaty, rather than an indefinite period, was also accepted to mollify several nations.

It was not until later in 1968 that Moscow and Washington attempted to meet the demand of India and others for protection against nuclear blackmail by proposing that the U.N. Security Council agree to call on its members for action in case of either such a threat or an actual attack. The two superpowers offered a U.N. Security Council resolution that welcomed their own intention to "provide or support immediate assistance, in accordance with the Charter, to any non-nuclear-weapon state party to the treaty on the non-proliferation of nuclear weapons that is a victim of an act or an object of a threat of aggression in which nuclear weapons are used."

The American statement of intent to go with that resolution, amounting to a formalization of Johnson's 1964 statement, said that "any state which commits aggression accompanied by the use of nuclear weapons or which threatens such aggression must be aware that its actions are to be countered effectively by measures to be taken in accordance with the United Nations Charter to suppress the aggression or remove the threat of aggression." Yet this procedure amounted to no new binding commitment by either of the superpowers since they, along with Britain, France, and Nationalist China, retain a veto in the Security Council against any action they might disapprove at such a crucial moment in the future.

Thus the nonnuclear nations, both those with a nuclear potential and those who lived in fear of their neighbors, continued to shy away from the treaty, offering one excuse or another. Nationalism and national interest remained strong, and these nations simply did not want to sign away the option of eventually joining the nuclear club themselves.

Furthermore, reports of a new development in the long search for a cheaper method of producing nuclear material for peaceful uses produced Soviet charges that it could lead to such weapons in Germany. In March, 1969, Great Britain, the Netherlands, and West Germany agreed to build plants in Britain and Holland, but not in West Germany, to begin to produce nuclear material by the new gas centrifuge process.

The two superpowers finally found themselves in general agreement. But neither was able to convince many of the other important nations that signing the treaty would be in their own interests.

In one of those bursts of activity that seem to occur at the end of long discussions, Soviet-American agreement on the draft treaty was finally reached at 4:25 A.M. in Geneva on January 18, 1968. But minor changes still had to be agreed to by the two superpowers before they felt confident enough to submit the treaty for the signatures of all nations on July 1. But the end of 1969, the treaty had been signed by three nuclear powers—the United States, the Soviet Union, and Great Britain—but only Great Britain had finalized the ratification process.

Another agreement attained during the Johnson years, although not directly by American action, was the Latin American Nuclear Free Zone Treaty. The idea of creating such a zone for areas like Latin America, Africa, Asia, and Antarctica, springs from a hope that such agreements would keep these areas free, at least to a major degree, of Soviet-American power rivalries by keeping them clear of the nuclear weapons of the superpowers and their allies. Such a preventative approach is similar to the agreements to ban the stationing of nuclear weapons in orbit or on the world's seabeds.

To date, however, only in Latin America has the free zone idea come to fruition and, even there, there have been difficulties. The treaty signed on February 14, 1967, at Tlatelulco, Mexico, by fourteen Latin American states was the culmination of five years of effort. Since then, eight other Latin American nations have signed, leaving only Cuba, which has refused to have anything to do with the scheme, and Guyana, whose eligibility has been in dispute.

The first of the key articles pledge the signatory nations to:

Use exclusively for peaceful purposes the nuclear material and facilities which are under their jurisdiction, and to prohibit and prevent in their respective territories:
(a) The testing, use, manufacture, production or acquisition by any means whatsoever of any nuclear weapons, by the Parties themselves, directly or indirectly, on behalf of anyone else or in any other way, and
(b) The receipt, storage, installation, deployment and any form of possession of any nuclear weapons, directly or indirectly, by the Parties themselves, by anyone on their behalf or in any other way.

The second key provision declares that the signatory nations "also undertake to refrain from engaging in, encouraging or authorizing, directly or indirectly, or in any way participating in the testing, use, manufacture, production, possession or control of any nuclear weapon." The treaty places all peaceful nuclear activities in the zone under the safeguard system of the IAEA.

The American interpretation, although it was not so stated by the signatory states, is that the treaty permits nuclear explosions for peaceful uses, such as digging a canal or harbor, but only by nations that have nuclear weapons and are asked to undertake such tasks. Brazil contended that the agreement should not inhibit Latin American countries from conducting such explosions, which it feared the treaty would do, and, with Argentina and Nicaragua, attached a protocol to the agreement. This protocol provides that, if in the future it should become technologically possible to create a nuclear explosive device that cannot be used as a weapon, the three nations will have the right to produce such a device. Technicians say that it is impossible to do so, however, because all explosive devices, including nuclear weapons, involve the same law of physics.

The free zone treaty also calls on nations outside the area but which have territories in the area to place these areas under the same restrictions—a reference to the remaining European colonial possessions and to American-controlled Puerto Rico, the Virgin Islands, and the Guantanamo Base at Cuba. This the United States has refused to accept. Washington did win an interpretation that there would be no bar to transit of nuclear weapons through Latin American territories en route to their destinations, which makes the Panama Canal available for transportation of such weapons.

On February 14, 1968, President Johnson agreed to another protocol on the non-use of nuclear weapons, adding that the United States "calls upon the powers possessing nuclear weapons" (meaning the Soviet Union) "not to use or threaten to use nuclear weapons against the Latin American states party to the treaty." However, the State Department indicated that the United States would not be bound by its pledge if a Latin American state received assistance, even in conventional arms, from a nuclear weapons state (i.e., if Cuba received such aid from the Soviet Union) for what was termed an armed attack. The memory of the Cuban missile crisis, plus the unresolved relationship between Havana and Washington, thus clouded the free zone treaty's total application.

All these agreements, affecting outer space and Latin America, were only peripheral to the major arms control effort of the Johnson Administration—the effort to begin negotiations on curbing the strategic arms race. There was however, a cumulative effect involved. The agreements, though minor compared to the central issue of curbing the strategic arms race, have served as building blocks. This has been true both in terms of Soviet-American negotiations over the agreements and in the internal discussions of the two governments, where each step, however small, had to be related to the whole of the problems of the nuclear years.

In retrospect, it is perhaps amazing that anything was accomplished in the arms control field, once President Johnson had escalated the war in Vietnam. To the Russians, the bombing of North Vietnam, a "fellow socialist country," was a source of great embarrassment. Furthermore, the Vietnam War accentuated, rather than diminished, the Peking-Moscow quarrel and the fight of the two Communist giants for a preponderant role in the world Communist movement. Those limited agreements which were reached in the Kennedy-Johnson period are testimony to the fact that a conjunction of interests is possible, even in periods of great strain between the two superpowers.

IV. The Mad Momentum

What is essential to understand here is
that the Soviet Union and the United
States mutually influence one another's
strategic plans.

Secretary of Defense
Robert S. McNamara
September 18, 1967

On the balmy evening of August 19, 1968, Secretary
of State Dean Rusk was host to a covey of ambassadors on a
cruise down the Potomac aboard the *Honey Fitz*. In a quiet
corner of the ship, Soviet Ambassador Anatoly F. Dobrynin told
Rusk what he had been waiting to hear.

The Kremlin had just agreed, said Dobrynin, to the summit
meeting President Johnson had been seeking with Premier Kosygin. It was expected that the two leaders would meet in Leningrad, and Johnson hoped to give a spectacular start to a series of
strategic arms limitation talks (SALT).

A few days earlier, Moscow had finally agreed to a date—
September 30—to begin the discussions. But both the September
30 date and the summit agreement were in vain. The day after
Dobrynin's message to Rusk, the Red Army invaded Czechoslovakia. In such a climate, the meetings were impossible.

The delay in strategic arms limitation talks may one day be
seen as a far greater tragedy for the world than the Soviet suppression of the liberal Communist movement of Alexander Dub-
cek in Czechoslovakia, for, at that moment, there appeared to be

79

a conjunction of interests and technologies that could have led to an important curb on the nuclear arms race. Undoubtedly, talks that fall, a Presidential election year, would have been difficult. The Republican candidate, Richard M. Nixon, by then was speaking of the "clear and present danger" of the Soviet missile buildup and calling for restoration of American military power to permit negotiation "from strength" and rejecting the idea of Soviet-American "parity" in the arms field in favor of American "superiority." But what transpired, both in the international political field and in missile and missile-defense development, was to make the problem infinitely more complex for the day when talks finally could begin.

The missile gap charges of the 1960 Presidential campaign had led to a massive American missile buildup. In 1967, Secretary of Defense Robert McNamara conceded that when Kennedy approved the buildup in 1961, the United States was acting out of uncertainty about Soviet intentions. "If we had had more accurate information about planned Soviet strategic forces," he said, "we simply would not have needed to build as large a nuclear arsenal as we have today." He readily conceded that American action, taken as a hedge against what was then only a theoretically possible Soviet buildup, could not have failed to bring a Soviet reaction.

It is now apparent that, after the 1962 Cuban missile crisis, the Kremlin laid the foundation for closing the missile gap by developing an anti-ballistic-missile system (ABM) and ordering a buildup in intercontinental ballistic missiles (ICBM's). By his clandestine effort to emplace missiles in Cuba in 1962, Khrushchev had daringly tried to close the gap in another fashion. The missiles he was putting in Cuba would not have altered the balance of power in numbers, but, had his short-cut method succeeded, it would have seriously endangered the American sense of security and given the Russians a psychological edge. But Kennedy forced Khrushchev to withdraw the missiles, and the episode very probably was one reason for Khrushchev's ouster in

1964. When the new leadership in the Kremlin began a longer-range effort to bring Soviet missilery at least to parity with that of the United States, the action-reaction phenomenon was clearly in play again.

Some time elapsed before Washington realized the sweeping importance of the Kremlin decision, however. What first came to major attention was what the Russians were doing in the anti-ballistic-missile (ABM) field, with American worries about these developments coming to a head in 1966. It was then that the path to the SALT talks first opened.

In November, during a visit to the LBJ Ranch in Texas, McNamara and General Earle G. Wheeler, chairman of the Joint Chiefs of Staff, explored with the President the alternatives to no agreement with the Soviet Union in the arms race. The result was Johnson's decision to approach Moscow about talks on limiting ABM systems in hopes that agreement would preclude the necessity for building an American system.

McNamara at that time had just completed the Pentagon's program of "assured destruction" of the Soviet Union if the Kremlin were to order a first strike at the United States. But he had rejected a host of other military programs as unnecessary. One was an anti-ballistic-missile system, which the Army had for years been pushing—first as Nike-Zeus and later as Nike-X.

Just what had transpired in Kremlin thinking is not totally clear. But it should be recalled that, in the 1960–62 period, while Khrushchev was still in power, there was evidence of Soviet deployment of an ABM system around the city of Leningrad. This development was enough to keep alive American ABM research, and in July, 1962, an ABM missile fired from Kwajalein atoll in the Pacific successfully intercepted a missile fired from Vandenberg Air Force Base in California. The problems of the ABM were many, however, and McNamara had stuck to research and development only, despite pressure from Congress to go ahead with deployment. Then, on November 7, 1964, barely three weeks after Khrushchev's ouster, what was thought to be a new ABM was displayed in Moscow's annual military parade. The United States and its allies gave this missile the code name Galosh. Its size suggested that it had a warhead big enough to render ineffective several American missiles descending in a cluster.

About the time of the Leningrad ABM defense reports, the United States, had begun to consider how to penetrate an anti-missile defense system. One idea was to use a single missile with several warheads. This new weapon, known as a MRV, or multi-ple-re-entry vehicle, had a nuclear buckshot effect, with a limited degree of predictable landing accuracy. Since 1962, such war-heads have been operational in the Polaris A-3 missile aboard American nuclear submarines, and by December, 1969, 28 of the 41 Polaris submarines were so equipped. Some years after the MRV development, the multiple warhead technique was refined into the multiple and independently targetable re-entry vehicle (MIRV). MIRV's are to be positioned atop Minuteman III ICBM's and on Poseidon C-3 submarine missiles. At the beginning of 1970, the American intention was to replace 510 of the 1,000 Minuteman I and II missiles with Minuteman III's and to replace the Polaris missile on 31 of the 41 missile submarines with the Poseidon C-3. First flight tests of these most advanced missiles took place in August, 1968. It appears, in retrospect, that the Soviet Union had reacted to the big American missile lead by beginning an ABM defense and that the United States, in turn, had reacted to the Soviet ABM defense by developing MRV's and later MIRV's. The Russians feared the U.S. lead might result in an American first strike capability that could wipe out the Russian missiles. The Americans feared a Soviet ABM defense system might negate the American lead and wanted a new way to pene-trate that defense lest the Russians thus achieve their own first strike capability—a capability simply to hit the other side a surprise blow, or "pre-emptive strike," of such intensity that the crippled victim cannot respond with any meaningful counterblow.

Such was the background of events against which, on Novem-

"Say, We Could Get Lost In This Thing"

—from *The Herblock Gallery* (Simon & Schuster, 1968)

ber 10, 1966, at the close of his conference with President Johnson in Texas, Secretary of Defense McNamara told newsmen that there was "considerable evidence" of Soviet "action . . . to initiate deployment of such [an ABM] system."

McNamara was talking about the Galosh, which by now was being emplaced around Moscow. The Leningrad system had come to a halt because, it was believed in the West, the Russian leaders had concluded that it would not be effective against American missiles. But Galosh was rated a far more important development, and the United States responded with McNamara announcing two decisions that had come out of the meeting at the LBJ ranch. A third he left unsaid.

The first was what he called the "possible production" of Poseidon, the new missile for Polaris submarines, the development of which had already been initiated "as an insurance program." The second was the conclusion that "it is much too early to make a decision for deployment" of an American ABM system against the coming Chinese missile threat and that "we have not arrived at a decision on any other deployment," i.e., on an ABM system to protect against Soviet missiles.

The third decision made at the LBJ Ranch did not surface for some time. It was to approach the Soviet Union in hopes of reaching agreement on a limitation of ABM deployments by both superpowers.

To get at this third objective, Johnson ordered Llewellyn E. Thompson, who was returning to Moscow for a second tour as American ambassador, to try to arrange talks on limiting ABM's. Thompson arrived in Moscow on January 11, 1967. The day before, in his State of the Union Message, Johnson had said that "the Soviet Union has in the past year increased its long-range missile capabilities. It has begun to place near Moscow a limited anti-missile defense." In his budget message on January 24, the President added that in fiscal year 1968 "we will continue intensive development of Nike-X but take no action now to deploy an anti-ballistic missile (ABM) defense" and "initiate discussions

with the Soviet Union on the limitation of ABM deployments."
He added that "in the event these discussions prove unsuccessful,
we will reconsider our deployment decision." Money was to be
provided in the new budget for such a contingency. On January
27, Johnson wrote Soviet Premier Kosygin proposing ABM talks.
But at the same time that the United States was asking the Soviet
Union to forego further ABM deployment, McNamara was saying that the United States had 1,446 land- and sea-based missiles,
compared to 470 for the Soviet Union. Furthermore, McNamara
hinted in his annual defense posture statement, presented to
Congress on January 23, that the United States was developing
new missiles to penetrate the Soviet ABM system. (The term
MIRV then was still classified. It was first revealed in the *Washington Post* on January 29.) In that statement, McNamara also
announced that acceleration of Poseidon development and production and deployment of the Minuteman III had been going
forward during the past year. The Poseidon would be produced
and deployed in the coming year, he said, and the number of
Minuteman III missiles would be increased.

These signs of American determination to continue a nuclear
lead and to counter the Soviet ABM must have been among the
reasons for a long period of internal discussion and delay in the
Kremlin in agreeing to the talks proposed by Johnson. Action-
reaction, again.

Pressures within the Johnson Administration and from Congress to go forward with an ABM program, if there could be no
agreement to limit rival ABM's, were accentuated by disagreement within the American intelligence community over what
came to be known as the Tallinn Line. This was a line of Soviet
radars stretching across the northwestern (as viewed from the
United States) approaches to the Soviet Union and in several
other places. Argument raged over what the Tallinn Line was for
almost two years before there developed a clear majority view
that the system was designed to protect against bombers, not
missiles.

On February 10, 1967, when he was visiting London, Kosygin was asked at a press conference about the American proposal for talks. In his answer, he justified a "defensive" weapons system this way: "Maybe an anti-missile system is more expensive than an offensive system, but it is designed not to kill people but to preserve human lives." Five days later, *Pravda* spelled out the Soviet position by saying that Kosygin had declared (although he had not) that "the Soviet Government was ready to discuss the problem of averting a new arms race, both in offensive and defensive weapons."

When Thompson was finally able to see Kosygin on February 18, it was quickly agreed that any talks would cover both offensive and defensive strategic nuclear weapons. Beyond that, Thompson could not get the Russians to move. On March 2, Johnson announced that he had had a reply from Kosygin saying that Moscow was willing to discuss "means of limiting the arms race in offensive and defensive nuclear missiles."

But the Soviet agreement to talk was only in principle. No date was suggested. Meanwhile, Moscow kept increasing its missile force, closing the gap with the United States. It was becoming evident in Washington that the Kremlin was building toward parity.

By the spring of 1967, McNamara, Air Force Secretary Harold Brown, and others were quietly trying out the idea that parity, or something close to it, would really make no difference, since the United States had so many nuclear weapons in one form or another that it would have the "assured destruction capability" necessary to deter a Soviet first strike. At a congressional hearing, Brown said that "our plans are that five years from now we will have just about as many missiles as we have right now." He added that the Russians

have known that. They have known it for a couple of years, and they keep on building. Now we can afford to let them build for a while, if they feel they want to catch up. But there is evidence that if we stop, they don't necessarily stop. They haven't stopped. I think that in our position we can afford to let this go on for a while, without overresponding.

During the same period, Soviet military leaders were boasting of their ability to knock down any incoming American missiles. "If missiles fly," said one general, "they will never arrive in Moscow. Detecting missiles in time and destroying them in flight are no problem today."

At the Glassboro summit conference in June, Johnson pressed Kosygin for a date to start the talks, and McNamara pressed his case on the disadvantage to both superpowers in deploying ABM systems. But Kosygin said he could not then set a date. The President concluded that this answer reflected a disagreement in the Kremlin—probably related to what he sensed was Kosygin's obsession with China.

Meanwhile, there had been other developments.

Three months earlier, in a moment of indiscretion in a drawing room of the governor's mansion in Nashville, Tennessee, before 125 educators, government officials, and newsmen, President Johnson had said:

> I wouldn't want to be quoted on this—but we've spent $35 or $40 billion on the space program. And if nothing else had come out of it except the knowledge we've gained from space photography, it would be worth ten times what the whole program has cost.
>
> Because, tonight, we know how many missiles the enemy has. And, it turns out, our guesses were way off. We were doing things we didn't need to do. We were building things we didn't need to build. We were harboring fears we didn't need to harbor.

In 1962, after Fidel Castro had refused to permit ground inspection in Cuba to determine that all Soviet missiles had been withdrawn, President Kennedy had foreshadowed this moment when he said, "The camera, I think, is actually going to be our best inspector." So it has become.

Supplemented by electronic snooping devices, the satellite

cameras used for surveillance by both the Americans and the
Russians have radically altered the range and nature of information available on nuclear energy activities. The huge increase of
American missiles in the early 1960's had been the result of misinformation on what the Russians were up to. When the buildup
began, the United States' spy-in-the-sky program had been relatively primitive. But by the time of Johnson's remarks, technical
innovations, such as cloud cover sensors to prevent wasting film,
had overcome most of the deficiencies. By the mid-1960's, Mc-
Namara was publicly reporting with confidence exact numbers of
Soviet missiles.

The American spy-in-the-sky program was openly talked
about by the Pentagon when it began, but by 1964 even the code
names had been labeled top secret. Nonetheless, the public caught
dramatic glimpses of the effectiveness of satellite photography
for the first time during the 1965 8-day flight of Gemini-5. Pictures of the earth from space left little doubt of the camera's
capability. Officials who know say that in pictures taken from
about 100 miles up, experts can distinguish with precision missile
and ABM sites, submarine construction pens, vehicles, individuals,
and even smaller objects of military interest. The remarkable
clarity is due, in part, to stereo photography, in which double
cameras provide a third dimension for the photo interpreter. The
program, still surrounded by secrecy, is believed to be two-part:
area surveillance satellites that orbit for three to four weeks and
close-look satellites that stay up about five days to rephotograph
objects of interest in the area pictures. The film capsules, ejected
from the satellites, descend by parachute and are recovered by
American aircraft in the Hawaiian area.*

In an article in *Aviation Week and Space Technology* on
September 15, 1969, Philip J. Klass reported that the U.S. area

---

* The story of SAMOS, the first spy-in-the-sky satellite was told in an
article by Howard Simons and Chalmers M. Roberts in the *Washington
Post* on December 8, 1963. It was later reprinted in *The New Front Page*,
by John Hohenberg, Columbia University Press, 1966.

surveillance satellites orbit for three to four weeks and the close-look satellites orbit for no more than five days before the film is recovered. He estimated by extrapolation from known data that "since early 1966, the U.S. has orbited 8–9 of the smaller photoreconnaissance satellites per year, with virtually no overlap between successive spacecraft" and that during this period there had been "an area-surveillance type spacecraft in orbit during approximately half of the days in the year." The Soviet Union, he estimated, "has achieved comparable days-in-orbit coverage since 1966–67 by launching more than 20 of its eight-day satellites per year."

The rival Soviet spy-in-the-sky program is conducted with Cosmos satellites, which provide, among other material, such intelligence information as the precise location of American missiles, which is vital for targeting. Soviet confidence in their system can be judged from the fact that in November, 1963, during discussions on the treaty to assure the peaceful uses of outer space, the Russians dropped their insistence on a ban on observation satellites. At that point, the Russians had launched only ten or eleven Cosmos satellites. (By December 31, 1969, they had launched 145 photographic satellites; the best unofficial estimate of comparable American launchings as of the same date is 182.)

Despite astonishingly accurate surveillance from the skies, the camera can disclose only facts or clues to facts. It cannot probe the minds of men nor disclose what is on the drawing boards. The Johnson Administration knew what was being deployed and, in part, what was being developed in the Soviet Union, but it remained uncertain about how far the missile and ABM programs would go. Thus, the Administration sought, despite the information available, to protect the United States against the unknown intentions of the Kremlin by continuing its own weapons development and beginning an ABM program.

Although Johnson apparently had decided to go ahead with some sort of an ABM system by mid-1967, the decision was not announced until September 18 in a speech McNamara delivered before the United Press International Editors and Publishers Conference in San Francisco. On that date, to the surprise of most Americans, McNamara accepted, if he did not heartily endorse, the idea of a "thin" or minimal ABM designed to protect against Chinese missiles, which was enough to satisfy Johnson's need for an ABM to protect himself politically from Republican critics as well as from the hawks in his own Democratic Party.

McNamara's speech was replete with warnings against the uselessness of a "heavy" ABM system to protect against Soviet missiles. The Russians "would clearly be strongly motivated to so increase their offensive capability as to cancel out our defensive advantage" from such a system, he argued. The United States and the Soviet Union would end, after spending billions, "relatively at the same point of balance on the security scale that we are now." McNamara spoke of the missile talks then still impending, saying that if they should fail, both nations "would be forced to continue on a foolish and feckless course." He added, "There is a kind of mad momentum intrinsic to the development of all new nuclear weaponry."

He went on to state the dilemma of the day: "The plain fact of the matter is that we are now facing a situation analogous to the one we faced in 1961 . . . we are uncertain of the Soviets' intentions." His remark was testimony to the fear of the unknown in the action-reaction cycle and to the limitations of even such fine intelligence devices as reconnaissance satellites.

Still, there was no word from Moscow about starting the talks. McNamara stated that as of October 1, 1967, the Soviet Union had increased its ICBM launchers to 720 from only 340 a year earlier. They had also tested a fractional orbital weapon, dubbed FOBS.* Offsetting these offensive advances was the fact that

---

* On November 2, 1967, McNamara announced that the Soviet Union might have operational in 1968 a "fractional orbital bombardment system (FOBS)." Whereas ICBM's are launched on a ballistic trajectory going as high as 800 miles, FOBS is a satellite launched on a low orbital trajectory that rises 100 miles above the earth. Initially, the advantage of FOBS was its ability to avoid the American warning system by approaching the United

the majority of the American intelligence community, as Mc-Namara stated on January 22, 1968, had concluded that the Tallinn Line was not an ABM system.

The evidence is uncertain, but some experts guess that the announcement of the anti-Chinese "thin" ABM system, the Sentinel, was used in Kremlin debates as the rationale for stepping up deployment of the Soviet SS-9 missile program. This program apparently was designed to penetrate a "thick," or anti-Soviet, ABM system which, it may have been concluded in the Kremlin, the Americans would eventually construct despite McNamara's words. The SS-9 is a massive Soviet ICBM estimated by the United States to pack in a single warhead a nuclear punch of between 12 and 25 megatons in explosive power. The Russians, having developed rockets of great thrust, which had put them first in the space race for so long, were able to mount huge warheads. (Earlier American concentration on miniaturization techniques, packing a lot into a small space, had meant less megatonnage per missile, but more missiles.)

By the end of 1967, the United States still had a large lead in the number of missiles, but total Soviet megatonnage was estimated as already on a par or perhaps ahead of that of the United States. While McNamara kept arguing that mere megatonnage was meaningless, that it amounted to overkill, others demanded both more American missiles and an anti-Soviet ABM system, as well.

Not until June 27, 1968, did the Soviet Union, through Gromyko, announce that it was "ready for an exchange of opinion" on "mutual restriction and subsequent reduction of strategic

---

States from the south, a possibility since countered by the installation of additional warning devices.

McNamara said that the United States had studied, but rejected, development of an American FOBS. He indicated that such a weapon was less accurate than an ICBM. The Russians have continued to conduct FOBS tests, and American experts consider it a potential weapon against U.S. strategic bomber bases. Since FOBS presumably would be directed to its target before completion of an orbit, it is not considered to be in violation of the ban on weapons in orbit provided by the outer space treaty.

vehicles for the delivery of nuclear weapons—offensive and defensive—including anti-missile." Gromyko, speaking to the Supreme Soviet at the time, indicated, however, that the decision in principle for at least "an exchange of opinion" with the United States had been won over considerable opposition. He then said, "To the good-for-nothing theoreticians who try to tell us . . . that disarmament is an illusion, we reply: by taking such a stand you fall into step with the most dyed-in-the-wool imperialist reaction, weaken the front of struggle against it." Gromyko did not identify the nationality of the "theoreticians" but it is a Soviet technique to surface internal differences by such obtuse phraseology. This theme was to recur in another Gromyko speech on July 10, 1969, probably indicating that the opponents of talks still had not given in to the mid-1968 Kremlin decision.

Four days after Gromyko's 1968 speech, while presiding at the White House ceremonial signing of the nonproliferation treaty, Johnson announced agreement with Moscow "to enter in the nearest future into discussions on the limitation and reduction of both offensive strategic nuclear weapons delivery systems and systems of defense against ballistic missiles."

But the "nearest future" was not to be. Johnson pressed the Russians for a summit meeting with Kosygin to launch the SALT talks with fanfare. The final affirmative answer came on August 19, but was negated by the Soviet invasion of Czechoslovakia the next day.

Two other factors by now also had entered the picture.

The first was that both the Russians and the Americans were beginning to test their multiple-warhead weapons, although in 1968 the Russians slowed down what Defense Secretary Clark M. Clifford, McNamara's successor, called "the only positively identified Soviet ABM complex, that at Moscow."

The other factor was the American Presidential campaign. On October 24, Candidate Nixon charged the Democrats with "creating a security gap for America." He said that American superiority in ICBM's had "become only marginal" and that "the trend is that even this slight edge will soon be gone." In place of the Democrats' "peculiar, unprecedented doctrine called 'parity,'" Nixon promised "to restore our objective of clear-cut military superiority" in the "aggregate" rather than "competition weapon by weapon." After the Russian invasion of Czechoslovakia, he called for Senate delay in consenting to the nuclear nonproliferation treaty, with the result that it was not voted upon until after he became President.

Nevertheless, the Johnson Administration worked out a series of proposals for the SALT talks and urged Moscow to set a date, but without result. After Nixon's election and before his inauguration, ACDA chief Foster, at Johnson's request, tried but failed to convince the President-elect to support beginning the talks immediately. Nixon responded that Johnson remained President until January 20, and that he, Nixon, would assume no responsibility for whatever Johnson might do about the talks before then. Word of this response apparently reached Moscow and no doubt accounts for the Russian decision to delay until Nixon assumed the Presidency.

Five days before leaving office, Clifford challenged Nixon's campaign remarks about the disappearing American missile superiority. He projected that by the end of 1969, the Russians would have deployed over 1,000 ICBM's in protective silos, compared to the American force of 1,054.* At the end of Khrushchev's

---

* ICBM's are buried, in concrete silos, widely spaced from one another, to protect them against damage from a nuclear explosion within a certain distance. The harder the silo, that is, the more strengthened by concrete construction or by emplacement in rock areas rather than in earth, the better the protection. Against such defensive measures, the offense tries to increase the accuracy of its ICBM's to negate the protective action. Offensive measures, as of early 1970 at least, appear to be more effective than defensive measures. In a paper entitled "Advanced Strategic Missiles, A Short Guide," published by the Institute for Strategic Studies in London, Ian Smart wrote, "A 1 MT [megaton] nuclear explosion on a surface of ordinary soil will pile up debris over an area which extends about a quarter of a mile from the point of the explosion. Any missile silo within that circle will almost certainly be unable to eject its missile once the debris has been deposited." The Soviet SS-9 is expected to have quarter-mile accuracy.

regime, the Soviet Union had possessed about 200 ICBM launchers, only part of them in hardened silos. The Brezhnev-Kosygin regime had obviously closed the gap.

But numbers and megatonnage are not the only measures of capability. While the Russians were "moving vigorously to catch up with the United States at least in numbers of strategic missiles —both land-based and sea-based," said Clifford, "it also is apparent that they are still well behind us in advanced missile technology —accuracy, MIRV's and penetration aids." Accordingly, he added:

It is reasonable to conclude that even if the Soviets attempt to match us in numbers of strategic missiles we shall continue to have, as far into the future as we can now discern, a very substantial qualitative lead and a distinct superiority in the numbers of deliverable weapons and the over-all combat effectiveness of our strategic delivery forces.

On January 20, 1969, Richard Milhous Nixon became President. That same day in Moscow, a Soviet spokesman said of the missile talks that "when the Nixon Administration is ready to sit down at the negotiating table, we are ready to do so, too."

He added that an agreement "is quite feasible though not easy."

V. Moving to the Table

> After a period of confrontation, we are
> entering an era of negotiation. Let all
> nations know that during this Adminis-
> tration our lines of communication will
> be open. . . . I know that peace does not
> come through wishing for it—that there
> is no substitute for days and even years
> of patient and prolonged diplomacy.
>
> *President* RICHARD M. NIXON
> *January 20, 1969*

In 1958, when Dwight D. Eisenhower was in the White
House and Richard Nixon was his Vice-President, Eisenhower
wrote in a letter to the Kremlin leaders that the two superpowers
must deal with each other or "end up in the ludicrous posture of
our just glaring silently at each other across the table."

How the superpowers deal with each other over arms control
matters, however, cannot escape being affected by their political
relationships. The story of the rival schemes for general and complete disarmament (G and C in the experts' lingo) illuminates that
fact.

In September, 1960, after the Eisenhower-Khrushchev relationship had reached a total impasse in the wake of the U-2 affair and
the aborted Paris summit conference, the Soviet leader came to
the United Nations in New York, where he attempted to create
a new ruling "troika" of Communist, capitalist, and neutralist

heads for the world organization, indulged in picturesque fit of shoe-banging, and put forward a Soviet plan for total disarmament. American officials discounted the plan as a grandiose propaganda move. Eisenhower would have nothing to do with it. But President Kennedy, in August, 1962, while discussing with his U.N. envoy, Adlai Stevenson, the American position within the General Assembly for the coming year, accepted the importance, for propaganda purposes, of matching the Soviet proposal. Stevenson argued for, and Kennedy agreed to, the introduction of a G and C disarmament plan that would permit the United States to propose specific steps toward a general goal—a technique that Kennedy preferred. The Kennedy decision grew out of months of Soviet-American discussions, which had produced what was called an agreed set of principles, although the agreement was more semantic than real.

The American plan, like the Soviet proposal, provided for various stages of disarmament and covered nuclear and conventional weapons as well as military manpower. Not surprisingly, each scheme sought to protect national areas of strength to the last possible moment in an over-all disarmament plan.

After Khrushchev's overthrow in October, 1964, Russian interest in G and C plans quickly declined, and Moscow, like Washington, concentrated on specific issues in arms control. General and complete disarmament quite obviously represented far too big a bite for either nation, and it still does.

Through concentration on specifics, agreement had been reached, or nearly reached, on a number of issues when Richard Nixon came to the Presidency. Those achievements, and the negotiating experiences behind them, plus rapidly accelerating weapons development, made it imperative that the new President pick up where his predecessor had left off in the effort to curb the arms race.

In view of the progress made toward talks during the Johnson era and the Soviet statement of interest on Inauguration Day, Nixon faced the problem of devising a negotiating position and arranging for the talks. There were two key elements in the Nixon approach: the talks had to be fitted into a larger scheme of foreign policy, and the bargaining position had to be Nixon's own and not the legacy of the Johnson Administration. Thus, delay was inevitable.

At his first press conference, on January 27, 1969, Nixon said that he favored strategic arms talks but that "it is a question of not only when but the context of those talks." He said he took a position between those who would "go forward with such talks clearly apart from any progress in political settlement" and those who felt that "until we make progress on political settlements it would not be wise to go forward on any reduction of our strategic arms, even by agreement with the other side."

Therefore, said the President, it was his belief that "what we must do is to steer a course between those two extremes." He defined his course:

> What I want to do is to see to it that we have strategic arms talks in a way and at a time that will promote, if possible, progress on outstanding political problems at the same time—for example, on the problem of the Mid-East and on other outstanding problems in which the United States and the Soviet Union, acting together, can serve the cause of peace.

He clearly had the Vietnam War in mind, though he did not mention it.

This Nixon thesis came to be known as "linkage," although the word was assiduously avoided on the public record. The Russian reaction, quite expectedly, was negative, and there has been no evidence that the thesis has affected Moscow's position on either Vietnam or the Middle East.

At the same press conference, the President also altered his terminology in regard to the position from which he would bargain. When a reporter reminded Nixon of his campaign demands for nuclear "superiority" over the Soviet Union, the President replied, "I think the semantics may offer an inappropriate approach to the problem." He said he would settle for "sufficiency," a term used earlier by his national security adviser, Henry A. Kissinger. He added, "I think 'sufficiency' is a better term, actually, than either 'superiority' or 'parity.' " Five months later, a reporter asked Deputy Defense Secretary David Packard what the term "sufficiency" meant. "It means," replied Packard, "that it's a good word to use in a speech. Beyond that it doesn't mean a God-damned thing." In public relations terms, Packard may have been correct, but in terms of international relations, he was totally wrong.

The men in the Kremlin, especially since the advent of the nuclear age, have long sought American acknowledgment of Soviet parity with the United States, both parity in general, as befits a great power, and parity in nuclear arms—not only for psychological reasons but because of the importance of creating what Thomas W. Wolfe, in *Soviet Power and Europe: 1965–69*, called

> a climate of acknowledged parity favorable to the pursuit of many of [the Soviet Union's] more important foreign policy objectives. Besides permitting the Soviet Union to deal politically with the United States as a strategic equal, a parity situation could be expected to undermine the remaining European faith in America's pledges to defend Europe even at the risk of nuclear war [and to limit American willingness] to intervene militarily against Third World "national liberation" movements without the backup of a superior strategic posture to deter Soviet counter-moves.

That Nixon was indeed prepared to accept a posture of parity, whatever nomenclature might be used, was evident from his remark to the NATO ministers during his visit to Brussels on April 10, 1969: "The West does not today have the massive nuclear predominance that it once had, and any sort of broad-based arms agreement with the Soviets would codify the present balance."

As the Nixon era took shape, those most skeptical about coming to terms with Moscow on arms limitation began to suggest that the Russians were seeking more than parity in the nuclear field. The Communist doctrinal commitment, according to Wolfe, long has been to "the goal of quantitative and qualitative superiority, a goal often pushed into the background by stubborn realities but never foresworn." In Washington, there was talk by Secretary of Defense Melvin R. Laird of the Soviet SS-9 missile as a "first strike" weapon, a line of reasoning reminiscent of the Eisenhower period when there was fear of a "nuclear Pearl Harbor."

Each new Administration, especially if the President is of a different political party than his predecessor, launches what it calls a complete review of policy. Shortly after taking office, Nixon asked for an appraisal of the SALT proposals inherited from the Johnson Administration. When the review was complete, Nixon's program was said to be not very different from Johnson's. However, as the arms race continued on into 1970, the Nixon Administration had to make alterations in its program to take into account technological changes and to ensure a variety of options at the bargaining table.

In his first months in office, the President had to cope with more immediate issues than launching the strategic arms limitation talks. There was the Vietnam War, the Middle East crisis, a trip to Western Europe to reassure the Allies, and domestic issues of all kinds. Not until June 11 was the arms review complete enough for the Administration to suggest a July 31 date for the start of talks. By then, the Kremlin was apparently having serious second thoughts.

One of the issues Nixon faced was what to do about the Sentinel anti-ballistic-missile defense system proposed by Johnson and McNamara. On March 14, the President announced that he had trimmed down the program and renamed it Safeguard and that it would go forward as "a measured construction on an active defense of our retaliatory forces." Furthermore, he stated, "we believe the Soviet Union is continuing their ABM development." They were most likely "making substantially better second-generation ABM components" and "continuing the deployment of very large missiles with warheads capable of destroying our hardened Minuteman forces" (a reference to the Soviet SS-9 missiles). They had "been substantially increasing the size of their submarine-launched ballistic missile force" and also were developing their fractional orbital missile.

The Nixon decision was to provide "for local defense of selected Minuteman missile sites and an area defense designed to protect our bomber bases and our command and control authorities" as well as to "provide a defense of the continental United States against an accidental attack" and "substantial protection against the kind of attack which the Chinese Communists may be capable of launching throughout the 1970's."

The decision set off a great debate in the U.S. Senate and across the nation, culminating on August 6 in Senate approval of the Safeguard system by the margin of a single vote. A 50-50 tie on the most crucial of two roll-call votes failed to add to the bill an amendment that would have held up deployment of the system. (Amendments require a majority to carry.)

There were three main components to Nixon's decision to transform the Sentinel program into the Safeguard program and to the subsequent congressional and public debate: (1) the technical feasibility of the ABM system, (2) the additional money involved over a period of years in a military budget already under wide attack for consuming too much of the nation's resources, and (3) the effect a decision to deploy an ABM system might have on the expected arms talks with the Soviet Union.

The details of the technical feasibility argument were complex and much disputed, the central point being, then as now, that in the field of nuclear weaponry offensive capabilities have far outstripped defensive measures. Technical problems involved in the complex ABM system cited in the 1969 discussions still plague the program. Cost figures for the system, like those for so many other major weapons developments, both nuclear and nonnuclear, are apparently impossible to determine with any exactitude. These two factors have led many to believe that billions would be committed for a system of doubtful technical validity at the very moment that the national will seems to call for a reshaping of the country's priorities to give more emphasis to solving domestic problems.

The dominant issue, however, both within the Administration and in the congressional and public debate, was the potential effect of launching the Safeguard system at a moment when it appeared the United States and the Soviet Union, having reached a point of rough parity in nuclear weaponry, were about to meet to discuss how to curb the spiraling arms race. The compelling argument, both to the President and the Congress, was that approval of the beginning of the Safeguard system would add to the bargaining weight of the American position at the SALT talks. Those who took this view, including Nixon, accepted the necessity of trying for an agreement to curb the arms race, but they felt that the chances of success were probably not very great. Even if they were to succeed, it would take months, or more likely years, to reach any accord. In short, it would be too risky to put aside the ABM plans. If Johnson had not proposed the Sentinel system, if it had been Nixon who first had to decide whether to launch an American ABM system, the answer might possibly have been different. But Sentinel existed when Nixon came to office and thus already had a life of its own, which the new President and the Congress found it difficult to deny.

Nixon's decision, contained in his March 14, 1969, announcement of the Safeguard system, centered on two points: protection of America's land-based ICBM's against a direct attack by the Soviet Union and defense of the American people against a possible Chinese nuclear attack within the next decade. The first concern rested on a suspicion, later to grow into a widespread belief throughout the Administration, that the only conceivable reason the Soviet Union was building a large number of SS-9 missiles was to create a force that could destroy the land-based American missiles, including the 1,000 Minuteman missiles. Those most alarmed, taking what is known in military jargon as the "worst case" view, foresaw a potential Soviet first strike against the United States. Others, who took a more comprehensive view of Soviet-American relations, suspected that the Kremlin leaders hoped to create a situation in which the threat of a strike that could destroy all American land-based missiles would severely, if not fatally, limit the bargaining power of the American President. As to the potential Chinese threat, Nixon took the position in private conversation that he simply could not permit the possibility that his successor, a decade later, would have no instrument of protection against nuclear blackmail by Peking, a theme he was to enlarge upon in 1970.

The action-reaction phenomenon was evident again, and caution won the day in both the Administration and in Congress. To hold back on the ABM system, especially after Johnson had endorsed it, was considered too much of a risk. The only concession Nixon made to the opposition was to limit the extent of the ABM system and to promise to review, and possibly modify, his decision "as the threat changes, either through negotiations or through unilateral actions by the Soviet Union or Communist China." He insisted that the Safeguard program was not provocative, that the modifications in the Sentinel plans eliminated any reason for the Soviet Union to see it as "the prelude to an offensive strategy threatening the Soviet deterrent," and that the program provided "an incentive for a responsible Soviet weapons policy and for the avoidance of spiraling U.S. and Soviet strategic arms budgets."

As long as both the United States and the Soviet Union have nuclear weapons that each knows the other can deliver, the balance of terror is preserved by mutual deterrence. The introduction of rival ABM systems, however, if they were able to prevent the delivery of most if not all offensive missiles, would upset that balance to the degree that the defenses of one nation or the other would be superior in effectiveness. The initiation of the Soviet ABM system had produced cries of alarm in the United States; Moscow was moving to upset the balance. The beginnings of the

American ABM system must surely have produced a mirror-image reaction in the Kremlin. An effective ABM defense for one side alone would, given the offensive weapons already in place, produce the conditions in which a first strike would be a thinkable risk in military terms. Hence, Nixon argued, by limiting the Sentinel system, which, despite denials, some felt was a prelude to a "thick" system to provide complete protection for the American population, he was not moving to "an offensive strategy threatening the Soviet deterrent."

The Senate debate centered on the ABM, its technical feasibility, its cost, and whether it would upset the balance of terror on the eve of the arms talks. By the time the Senate voted, however, opponents of the Safeguard system had come to realize the importance of the other new scientific development, the multiple-headed, independently targetable warheads known as MIRV's. The congressional debate brought to light much new information on the MIRV, vital data for both American and Soviet consideration at the SALT talks.

MIRV was conceived in response to fears that a Soviet ABM system could provide a defense that American weapons with but a single warhead might not be able to penetrate. The strongest public proponent of MIRV development (and, indeed, of a whole spectrum of continuing efforts to assure American superiority) was Dr. John S. Foster, Jr., the Pentagon's research and engineering chief and former head of the University of California's Lawrence Radiation Laboratory at Livermore. Foster, referring to the Russians, declared that his aims were "to make sure that whatever they do of the possible things that we imagine they might do, we will be prepared."

While the Senate argued over the ABM issue and tried to determine the significance of MIRV, Foster and the Pentagon fought to continue and complete MIRV testing. When senators began to call for a MIRV test ban as a first order of business at the coming arms talks, Foster argued that "an effective limitation on Soviet ABM's should be a precondition to a ban on further

MIRV testing." He also cast doubt, in testimony before a House Foreign Affairs subcommittee on August 5, 1969, according to the public portion of the record, on the ability of the United States to police a MIRV test ban. To Foster, the American MIRV was designed as a second strike weapon—for a retaliatory blow only—to deter a Soviet first strike and therefore "must be considered as a stabilizing influence" in the arms race.

The Soviet Union was soon made aware by the American debate that a MIRV test ban might be the initial U.S. proposal at the talks. Furthermore, it may have been that many of the arguments in favor of the ban were found convenient by those in the Soviet Union who opposed a strategic missile agreement with the United States. That there continued to be such opponents could be deduced from Gromyko's July 10, 1969, speech, which undoubtedly reflected the will of the Kremlin majority. The arms race, he said, had long ago become a folly. Much else of what he said was reminiscent of reasoning in the United States:

There are problems connected with disarmament that require urgent solution. Among these problems, one of the most important is the problem of the so-called strategic arms. The point of the matter is primarily whether the big powers ought to come to an agreement to arrest the race of creating increasingly destructive means of attack and counterattack, or whether each of them is to try to break out ahead in one sphere or another to obtain military advantage against his rivals, which will force the latter to mobilize even greater national resources for the arms race; and thus ad infinitum.

There is another side of the matter, too, that also cannot be ignored by a state's long-term policy. It is linked to a considerable extent with the fact that the systems of the control and direction of arms are becoming increasingly autonomous, if one can put it this way, from the people who create them. Human capacity to hear and see are incapable of reacting to modern speeds. The human brain is no longer capable of assessing at sufficient speed the results of the multitude of instruments. The decisions adopted by man depend in the last analysis upon the conclusions provided by computers. The government[s] must do everything possible to be able to determine the development of events and not to find themselves in the role of captives of the events.

Once again Gromyko said the Soviet Union was ready for "an exchange of views" on arms limitations. But it was more than three months before talks began.

Meanwhile, scientific development raced on in both countries. By mid-1969, the United States had made nine flight tests of Poseidon submarine-borne missiles with MIRV warheads and nine tests of Minuteman III. The test program was scheduled to be completed in May, 1970, with first deployment following closely thereafter. The Soviet MRV and MIRV programs were thought in Washington to be somewhat less advanced. John S. Foster, Jr., said on August 5, 1969, that in his judgment the Soviet "triplet," (three bombs in a single warhead) "probably is a MIRV" designed to attack hard targets, namely American Minuteman missile sites. Furthermore, Foster assumed that the Russians "under normal circumstances would be ready to deploy the SS-9 triplet some time in the latter half" of 1970, a date not far beyond the completion date of the American schedule. Thus, by the fall of 1969, it appeared that the MIRV genie was out of the bottle. (Some officials said the genie had escaped as far back as 1962, when the Polaris A-3 missile, with a multiple but not independently targetable warhead, was first placed in service aboard an American submarine.)

Whether the American estimate of the Soviet MIRV development was overstated or understated, the gap itself may have played a part in the long Soviet delay in agreeing to start talks. Perhaps the Kremlin feared that it might be embarrassed by an American proposal at the talks for a quick freeze on further MIRV tests.

The action-reaction phenomenon once again was evident in MIRV development. Had the two superpowers met in the fall of 1968, at the time MIRV tests for Poseidon and Minuteman III missiles were about to get under way, they might have been able

"Shall We All Agree That There's No Hurry?"

—Copyright 1969 by Herblock in *The Washington Post*

to agree on a mutual freeze and thus have prevented escalation of the nuclear arms race to a new, more dangerous, and more expensive level. Whether the same results would have been obtained if the Nixon Administration had been willing to start talks just after the new President took office is debatable, but perhaps not impossible. But clearly, by the time the talks did begin, the problem had become far more complex.

The Nixon Administration did act quickly on one arms control issue. Shortly after taking office, the President gave the go-ahead to Senate consideration of the nuclear nonproliferation treaty, and consent was voted, 83 to 15, on March 13, 1969. However, Moscow withheld ratification, apparently waiting for the West Germans to sign, and the United States also delayed formal ratification in hopes of concluding the process on the same day as the Soviet Union.

The West German election in October, 1969, and the subsequent choice of Willy Brandt, head of the Social Democratic Party, as chancellor, finally broke the nonproliferation treaty logjam. Brandt, as foreign minister in the previous coalition government of Kurt Georg Kiesinger, had long advocated West German signature, but in vain. Once in office, Brandt signed the treaty in Bonn on November 28, and by prior agreement the United States and the Soviet Union completed their own ratification processes, leaving only the final act of depositing their ratifications.*

---

* In general, multilateral international agreements provide that one or more governments involved, usually major powers, will act as the depository (or depositories) of the document. In a physical sense, someone has to hold the document; in a diplomatic sense, there must be some specified place to which nations can direct messages affecting such an agreement, for example, either to join an existing treaty or to serve notice the document is no longer considered binding. In the United States (where the physical depository is a State Department vault), the common belief is that the Senate ratifies a treaty, but this is not technically correct. The Constitution provides that the Senate shall give its "consent" by a two-thirds vote of those present. The President then signs the instrument of consent and, finally, deposits the ratification document. Only when that last step has been taken is the treaty binding on the United States, assuming that by then it has had the number

Brandt, however, issued a statement saying that the German signature on the document was based on several understandings, among them that the U.N. resolution calling on its members for action in case of either a nuclear threat or an actual attack applied without restriction to West Germany, even though that country is not a U.N. member. Furthermore, West Germany pointed out that the treaty provided an eighteen-month period for melding the IAEA-Euratom inspection provisions. Until that step had been completed, West Germany would not ratify the treaty.

Nonetheless, the West German signature, plus Brandt's new and more friendly policy toward the Soviet Union and Eastern Europe, had increased the treaty's prospects. Japan, for example, signed in February, 1970, lest it lose the opportunity afforded signatory nations to play a role in formulating the inspection provisions.

On March 5, 1970, when the required forty nonnuclear nations had completed ratification, including deposit of their ratifications in Moscow, London, or Washington, the United States and the Soviet Union made their deposits, and the treaty at last came into force. Still, it lacked adherence from such important nuclear-potential nations as Australia, Israel, Japan, India, and Pakistan.

Nixon's general review of American post-Vietnam policy in Asia produced a new doctrine in the broad area of nuclear protection for nonnuclear nations. The new doctrine was disclosed by the President on July 25, 1969, during a stop at Guam en route to Asia. He said then that in the future Asian nations would be expected to take primary responsibility for their own military defense with a single stated exception: the threat of a major power involving nuclear weapons. An anonymous White House spokesman (identified as Henry A. Kissinger) later added that

---

of final approvals by other nations required to bring it into force. The final two steps—signing and depositing the document—are usually *pro forma* but they can be used, as in the case of the nonproliferation treaty, for purposes of delay.

the Administration would have to take into account the nature of the threat to any nation, so that a threat with nuclear weapons would have to be treated with a special gravity, whether or not a formal American commitment to such a nation existed.

Nixon's remarks at Guam could not be directly quoted, but he later put the most important phrases on public record. In his 1970 report to Congress on "United States Foreign Policy for the 1970's," he formulated the doctrine this way: "We shall provide a shield if a nuclear power threatens the freedom of a nation allied with us, or of a nation whose survival we consider vital to our security and the security of the region as a whole."

But these generalities, which left the initiative in the hands of the United States, were no more satisfactory to the nuclear-potential nations that had not acceded to the nonproliferation treaty than had been the joint Soviet-American pledges at the United Nations.

Technical arguments, the issue of on-site inspection, and the continuing arms race itself have thus far prevented agreement on extending the 1963 nuclear test ban treaty so as to include underground explosions. Since that treaty took effect, the U.S. Atomic Energy Commission has announced a total of 173 weapons-related American underground tests through December 31, 1969. The AEC also announced that its detection network had disclosed, in the same period, three Soviet underground tests and thirty-four seismic signals, which presumably represented tests. However, not all tests of either nation are announced by the AEC. To do so would disclose the degree of sophistication of the American detection system. (In the same period, the AEC reported two British underground tests, thirteen French atmospheric tests, and one Chinese underground and nine Chinese atmospheric tests.)

Once above-ground testing had been banned, American and Soviet scientists developed techniques to try out devices both more powerful and, as in the case of ABM and MIRV testing, more sophisticated than had previously been carried out underground. Thus the test ban, while protecting the world's population from most of the contamination resulting from atmospheric testing, did not, as some of its proponents had hoped, inhibit the arms race itself. In a few of these underground tests, in both the Soviet Union and the United States, some radioactive debris escaped into the atmosphere and drifted into Canada from the United States and into China and Japan from the Soviet Union. Both Moscow and Washington, although they exchanged formal notes for the record, avoided charges of violation of the test ban treaty and proclaimed that the venting (as it was called) was unintentional and harmless to humans.

Detection devices to monitor underground tests have improved over the years, but not to the point that the United States was prepared to accept the Soviet proposal for an underground ban without on-site inspection. Third countries, notably Sweden, have tried to develop compromise techniques, but to no avail. Sweden proposed a challenge-and-response system under which the nation suspecting a violation would challenge the other to disprove it, perhaps by on-site inspection, and be permitted to withdraw from the treaty if it found the response unsatisfactory. Another proposal was to ban the larger underground tests and limit tests to a specific level as measured on the internationally accepted seismic scale.

After leaving his post as head of the U.S. Arms Control and Disarmament Agency, William C. Foster declared, "The time has come for a hard look at the necessity for on-site inspections." In a speech on October 8, 1969, he argued for a comprehensive test ban (CTB):

It is hard to believe that the security risk posed by the relatively few tests the Soviets might be able to carry out without being detected by national means would exceed the security risk of unlimited numbers of Soviet weapons tests that are permitted in the absence of a CTB. Of course, it can be pointed out that without a CTB the U.S. also could continue testing and thereby counterbalance the Soviet tests. But would this really counterbalance the security risk or would it merely add fuel to the nuclear arms race?

Foster, with the luxury of having shed public responsibility, gave voice to the internal arguments in which he had so long been involved when he said that "the crux of the problem is how much assurance is adequate, and this is a political rather than a technical decision." So far, the rule of thumb has prevailed: where there is technical doubt, political decisions tend to be on the conservative side.

In October, 1969, the United States and the Soviet Union reached an additional agreement on a pre-emptive step to avoid enlarging the locale of the arms race by ensuring that the world's seabeds be reserved for peaceful purposes only. The effort to reach this agreement, initiated in 1967, had followed the pattern of the successful effort to ban nuclear weapons from outer space.

Although both Washington and Moscow readily agreed to the principle of the treaty, each sought to protect its own interests in the final document. The Soviet Union called for complete demilitarization, a ban inclusive enough to preclude not only nuclear weapons emplaced on seabeds but also defensive mines and various submarine detection devices that the United States already had emplaced to track the expanding Soviet underwater fleet. The United States proposal was limited to a ban on nuclear weapons and other weapons of mass destruction (specifically, chemical and biological weapons). In mid-August, 1969, the Russians offered to accept the American version of the treaty if the United States would accept the Soviet proposal that the ban become effective at the 12-mile offshore limit rather than at the 3-mile limit Washington had proposed.

By fall, an agreement satisfactory to Washington and Moscow had been reached, but other nations had become disturbed about their rights under the rather generalized inspection provisions and about the effects of the offshore limitation on certain coastal areas. The inspection agreement in the draft treaty permitted any nation to check for itself the international waters covered, a task so difficult that probably only the United States and the Soviet Union could or would undertake it. The U.N. General Assembly expressed these feelings on December 12, 1969, when it asked the two drafting powers to clear up the uncertainties when they next met at the Geneva Disarmament Conference in 1970.

While Washington waited for Soviet word on when and where to start the SALT talks, the Sino-Soviet conflict appeared to be approaching the point of warfare.

A word should be said here about China, which has become increasingly important in the nuclear calculations of both the United States and the Soviet Union. The Chinese nuclear weapons and missile tests, monitored by American observation satellites and other means, have shown a high degree of technical sophistication. Although, by 1969, the program lagged behind American estimates, John S. Foster, Jr., Pentagon research chief, said on February 24, 1970, that a Chinese test of an ICBM could be expected within the year.

Exactly what the Russians knew or thought about the Chinese program is unknown, but Red Army marshals have clearly grown increasingly worried about China's nuclear growth, especially in light of the intensifying Sino-Soviet political controversies and the recent military clashes along the two countries' long common borders. Some analysts have even suggested that the Soviet ABM system was designed in part to protect against Chinese missiles. This view was acknowledged indirectly by the Nixon Administration when Henry A. Kissinger, in an interview in *Look* magazine on August 12, 1969, stated, "I doubt if the Soviet Union will give up the Moscow (ABM) system, and I doubt I would urge them to."

Although the record shows that the Chinese Communists have acted in a generally prudent manner militarily since coming to power, their excessively bellicose language has engendered fears. It is not easy to dismiss totally, for example, the widely printed Chinese polemic of 1960 in which Peking professed no fear of nuclear war with the United States and declared that the inevitable Communist victory "would create very swiftly a civilization thousands of times higher than the capitalist system and a truly beautiful system for [the Communists] themselves." Mao Tse-tung and his followers, verbally at least, have consistently rejected Khrushchev's warning that, although the United States may be a paper tiger, as Peking has claimed, "the paper tiger has nuclear teeth."

In September, 1969, when relations between the Soviet Union and China had reached a new high point of tension, the accident of death brought Kosygin to Hanoi for the funeral of Ho Chi Minh, the leader of North Vietnam. The Soviet leader then made a quick trip to Peking, where he met with Chinese Premier Chou En-lai. After the meeting, it was announced that the two nations would meet to talk over their border quarrel on October 20, 1969.

To Washington's surprise, on the day the Sino-Soviet talks began, Soviet Ambassador Dobrynin met President Nixon secretly at the White House. A few days later, on October 25, a joint announcement was made of the date—November 17—and the place—Helsinki, Finland—for preliminary discussions of negotiations on curbing the strategic arms race.

The coincidence of dates for the beginning of the Moscow-Peking talks and the Dobrynin call on Nixon added to the American conviction that one of the reasons for the Kremlin's delay in agreeing to the SALT talks had been to avoid jeopardizing the chances of resolving the quarrel with China. The Soviet leaders long had been aware of Peking's charges that Moscow and Washington were acting in collusion against China. The Soviet leaders had also been wary of signs that the Nixon Administration was beginning to relax American hostility toward the Peking regime. The Chinese, in turn, played upon Soviet worries by agreeing in December, 1969, to resume the Chinese-American diplomatic dialogue that Peking had broken off two years earlier. It was evident, as the 1970's began, that the triangular Washington-Moscow-Peking relationship would be critical in world affairs in general and in relation to arms control measures in particular.

On the day of the Washington-Moscow announcement of the

SALT talks, Secretary of State William P. Rogers sought to bury the Nixon "linkage" thesis—anathema to Moscow—by telling a press conference that the SALT talks "are not conditional in any sense of the word. We haven't laid down any conditions for those talks." But the Administration hedged when Nixon's press secretary, commenting on the Rogers statement the following day, stated that "these talks cannot take place in a vacuum. The President's feeling is that there is a certain relation between SALT and outstanding political problems." Moscow expressed annoyance but nothing more.

At his press conference, Rogers also did what so many secretaries of state before him had done when American-Soviet talks were announced: he warned against "euphoria" and predicted long and difficult discussions. He also noted that the Moscow-Washington announcement had referred to negotiations "on curbing the strategic arms race," not on disarming the two superpowers. Rogers pointed out that Peking's nuclear program had not progressed far enough to require China to join the talks. If the two superpowers could reach agreement, he added, "We can deal with China's problem later on."

Announcement of the date for the SALT talks brought renewed congressional and public pressure on Nixon to propose at Helsinki a mutual freeze on MIRV testing while the discussions were under way, in hopes that such a step would lead to a permanent ban, perhaps in connection with a ban or limitation on rival ABM systems. But the President, on the eve of the talks, ruled out any such proposal. Indeed, the United States secretly tipped off the Soviet Union that there would be no American proposals, and Washington expressed the hope that there would be none from Moscow either. This turned out to be the case. Nixon wanted instead an exchange of views in order to define the scope of the more substantive talks to follow the preliminaries at Helsinki. In Washington, caution was the order of the day, and the same appeared to be true in Moscow.

To head the American delegation, Nixon named Gerard C.

Smith, whom he had also selected to succeed William C. Foster as head of the Arms Control and Disarmament Agency. Smith had been a State Department official in the Eisenhower years and a leading advocate of the ill-fated multilateral nuclear force. He now found himself in the position of his predecessors, pushing for Presidential approval of risk-taking, in contrast to those who advocated a cautious approach to arms control. The four other American delegation members were Paul H. Nitze, who had served as Deputy Secretary of Defense in the last years of the Johnson Administration; Llewellyn E. Thompson, the retired Ambassador to the Soviet Union, who had tried to get the SALT talks under way for Johnson; Harold Brown, formerly head of the Lawrence Radiation Laboratory, chief of Pentagon research, and Secretary of the Air Force, and at present President of the California Institute of Technology; and Major General Royal B. Allison, representing the Joint Chiefs of Staff, who, during the previous year, had immersed himself in the nuclear arms control problem.

The Soviet delegation was comparable. It was headed by Deputy Foreign Minister Vladimir S. Semyonov, the top Moscow expert on Germany. He was picked in place of the top Soviet arms control expert, V. V. Kutzenov, who was then leading the Soviet delegation at the Peking talks. Sitting on Semyonov's right at the Helsinki table was Colonel General Nikolai V. Ogarkov, First Deputy Chief of the General Staff (the Soviet equivalent of the American Joint Chiefs). On Semyonov's left was Dr. Alexander N. Shchukin, a scientific academician. In all, the Soviet group of 6 delegates and 18 advisers included 5 generals, an admiral, and 2 colonels. The American group of 5 delegates and 19 advisers had only 1 general and 3 field-grade officers. Each group included many who had lived in the other group's country and spoke its language; many had long been associated with arms control.

At the single public session in Helsinki, both sides spoke of hopes for "mutually acceptable" limitations on the arms race. In a message to the conference, Nixon repeated his concept of "sufficiency," declaring that he did not "underestimate the suspicion and distrust that must be dispelled if you are to succeed in your assignment." He alluded to his linkage theory by saying that he was "conscious of the historical fact that wars and crises between nations can arise not simply from the existence of arms but from clashing interests or the ambitious pursuit of unilateral interests. That is why we seek progress toward the solution of the dangerous political issues of our day."

The latter statement indicated, once again, how intertwined in the President's thinking about arms control were Soviet-American relationships affecting the Middle East, Vietnam, and the East-West problem in Europe.

The atmosphere at international conferences, especially at strictly Soviet-American meetings, usually provides a clue to what is occurring behind closed doors. During the five weeks of the Helsinki meeting, there were constant reports by both sides of "business-like" sessions without polemics, interspersed with social events at which smiles and clinking champagne glasses were the order of the day. The end result, publicly, was a December 22, 1969, communiqué. This was the key paragraph:

> The preliminary exchange of views which took place concerning the limitations of strategic arms was useful to both sides. As a result of that exchange, each side is able better to understand the views of the other with respect to the problems under consideration. An understanding was reached on the general range of questions which will be the subject of further U.S.-Soviet exchanges.

The two nations agreed to resume negotiations on April 16, 1970, in Vienna and to return at an unspecified date to Helsinki. The Vienna talks, as was the case at Helsinki, were to alternate between the Soviet and American embassies, thus providing a degree of secrecy satisfactory to both countries.

It appeared that at Helsinki the two sides accepted the idea of mutual deterrence—hopefully at the existing rough parity of nuclear arms. Each sought to learn how the other approached the problem and how various weapons systems, including ABM's and MIRV's, were viewed within the context of the deterrence concept. The exchanges—usually in the form of working papers read by one side to the other at the conference table and expanded on in private social conversations—were both preliminary and philosophical rather than detailed. This was made evident by the post-Helsinki feeling expressed privately by American and Soviet officials that the Vienna round of talks would have to get down to specific proposals by each side if there were to be any agreement in 1970.

On the American side, the NATO allies, as Nixon had pledged, were told what had transpired at Helsinki. Still, as 1970 began, many of these nations, with the exception of Great Britain and perhaps France, had not, in Washington's view, realized the significance of a potential agreement based on a rough Soviet-American parity in place of the long-held American nuclear superiority. Whether this realization would lead to a feeling among Western European countries that the United States—because of the increased danger to itself—would be less willing to come to their aid in the future than it had in the past remained to be seen.

One of the uncertainties at Helsinki concerned Soviet intentions in building so many massive SS-9 ICBM's. By February 20, 1970, according to Secretary of Defense Melvin R. Laird, the Soviet Union had deployed or had under construction over 275 SS-9's. Other officials estimated that, at the current rate of deployment, the figure would approach 400 by the fall of 1970.

An official American projection issued on February 18, 1970, estimated that by the end of the year the Soviet Union would have 1,290 ICBM's, compared to 1,054 for the United States, and 300 submarine-launch ballistic missiles, compared to 656 for the United States. The President expressed concern about the multiple warhead program for the SS-9 and about the Soviet Union's "apparent interest" in improving ICBM accuracy.

In megatonnage, or what is sometimes called "throw weight" (what one side can hurl at the other), the Soviet Union was considerably ahead in terms of land-based missiles.

Moscow's potential for adding MIRV warheads to its SS-9's and for creating a force of mobile, land-based missiles ("easily camouflaged" and "hardly detected by [American] air and space reconnaissance," as the commander of the Soviet Strategic Rocket Forces had boasted in early 1968) added to worries in Washington on the eve of the Vienna meeting.

Exactly what developments produced counterpart worries in Moscow can only be surmised; certainly the far larger American nuclear submarine fleet and the apparently greater American progress in MIRV testing were among such worries. One about which there was no doubt was the development of the American Safeguard ABM system.

On January 30, 1970, President Nixon announced at a press conference that he had decided, after a review, to proceed with the Safeguard system. The first phase, begun after congressional approval in mid-1969, was deployment of the ABM system to protect two complexes of Minuteman missiles, one at Malmstrom Air Force Base in Montana, and the other at Grand Forks Air Force Base in North Dakota. The President indicated at his press conference, that the first phase was to be enlarged and completed, and the second phase was to be initiated, but he did not disclose any details.

On February 24, Laird announced the new program. He called for congressional authorization of an additional Safeguard site at Whiteman Air Force Base in Missouri and of advance preparation work on five more sites, but without a commitment for deployment. The five new sites were to be located in the northeast, the northwest, the Washington, D.C., area, the Michigan-Ohio area, and at Warren Air Force Base in Wyoming. Laird called this "modified phase II" Safeguard program a minimum effort and added that he believed it to be the only viable course, "given

President Nixon's determination to postpone additional actions on U.S. offensive systems this year in order to advance prospects for success at SALT."

Nixon, in January, repeated the two major reasons he had given the previous March for fashioning the Safeguard system: protection of the American ICBM force from Soviet attack and defense of the general population against the possibility of a Chinese attack a decade hence. In speaking of China, Nixon said that, within ten years, "It will be very important for the United States to have some kind of defense so that nuclear blackmail could not be used against the United States" (or its Pacific allies). He appeared to be thinking of the effect his Guam doctrine— the pulling back of conventional American military power— would have on the balance of power in Asia. Thus he argued that the Safeguard system would give the United States "a credible foreign policy in the Pacific it otherwise would not have."

The Nixon decision, with the second round of the SALT talks impending, set off a new round of congressional and public debate on the Safeguard system, the MIRV program, and their relationship to a possible strategic arms limitation agreement with the Soviet Union.

The problems ahead in arms control were highlighted on February 18 in the President's report to Congress on United States foreign policy for the 1970's. He informed Congress and the nation, "We are now entering an era in which the sophistication and destructiveness of weapons present more formidable and complex issues affecting our strategic posture." He found a serious threat to the retaliatory capability of the United States in the growing forces of Soviet missiles, land- and sea-based, with greater accuracy and with multiple warheads. He suggested three categories of proposals for the SALT talks that would enable the United States to respond to a broad range of Soviet proposals: a limitation on the numbers of missiles, limitations on the capabilities of missiles, and a reduction in offensive forces.

The dilemma Nixon faced in his efforts to design strategic forces for the 1970's was described in these words:

> I recognize that decisions on shaping our strategic posture are perhaps the most complex and fateful we face. The answers to these questions will largely determine whether we will be forced into increased deployments to offset the Soviet threat to the sufficiency of our deterrent, or whether we and the Soviet Union can together move from an era of confrontation to one of negotiation, whether jointly we can pursue responsible, non-provocative strategic arms policies based on sufficiency as a mutually shared goal or whether there will be another round of the arms race.

Two days later, Defense Secretary Laird told Congress that the Soviet Union was continuing rapid deployment of major strategic offensive weapons systems at a rate that could, by the mid-1970's, "place us in a second-rate strategic position with regard to the future security of the free world." Laird announced a military budget for fiscal 1971 that was designed to preserve a range of options for the development of new systems—land-based and, perhaps, mobile missiles, a new submarine missile system, a new manned bomber—all of which, he indicated, would be necessary unless there was progress at the SALT talks. In announcing his budget, Laird once again expressed the gnawing American fear:

> Because the Soviet Union is a closed society, they can conduct their military research and development programs behind a thick veil of secrecy, making it very difficult for us to assess their progress in a timely manner. . . . We simply do not have enough knowledge to assess the threat properly. The only prudent course is to advance our knowledge at a reasonable pace in every area of significance to our future military strength.

As the April 16 date for reconvening the SALT talks in Vienna approached, the bold and the fearful in Washington, in and out of the Administration, began to put pressure on the President. Some wanted him to make only cautious proposals at the talks;

others wanted him to suggest a moratorium on MIRV and ABM deployment, as well as a freeze of ICBM's at the current level. From Moscow came charges that many in the United States, and especially Laird, did not seem to want to curb the arms race at all. It was the familiar mood music that always precedes a serious Soviet-American conference.

The technical problems inherent in any agreement would be intricate. But the essential fact is that the decision leading to agreement would be political. Once again, an American President faced the splendid isolation of the White House at a fateful moment in history. And far away, in Moscow, where there were no prying newsmen or obstreperous legislators to reveal the internal arguments in the Kremlin, the Soviet leaders faced the same critical moment.

Thus, the decade of the 1970's began in hope and fear, in action and reaction. What had been true for a quarter of a century was still true. If a nuclear holocaust was to be avoided, each side was compelled by the stark facts of the nuclear age to talk with the other side; yet each was consumed with doubts about the other's intentions, doubts that induced extreme caution in both Washington and Moscow. But the fundamental truth remained. As President Johnson had put it, on August 26, 1966, "Uneasy is the peace that wears a nuclear crown."

The Baruch Plan

Statement by Bernard M. Baruch, United States Representative to the United Nations Atomic Energy Commission, June 14, 1946

MY FELLOW MEMBERS OF THE UNITED NATIONS ATOMIC ENERGY COMMISSION, AND MY FELLOW CITIZENS OF THE WORLD:

We are here to make a choice between the quick and the dead. That is our business.

Behind the black portent of the new atomic age lies a hope which, seized upon with faith, can work our salvation. If we fail, then we have damned every man to be the slave of Fear. Let us not deceive ourselves: We must elect World Peace or World Destruction.

Science has torn from nature a secret so vast in its potentialities that our minds cower from the terror it creates. Yet terror is not enough to inhibit the use of the atomic bomb. The terror created by weapons has never stopped man from employing them. For each new weapon a defense has been produced, in time. But now we face a condition in which adequate defense does not exist.

Science, which gave us this dread power, shows that it *can* be made a giant help to humanity, but science does *not* show us how to prevent its baleful use. So we have been appointed to obviate that peril by finding a meeting of the minds and the hearts of our people. Only in the will of mankind lies the answer.

It is to express this will and make it effective that we have been assembled. We must provide the mechanism to assure that atomic energy is used for peaceful purposes and preclude its use in war. To that end, we must provide immediate, swift, and sure punishment of those who violate the agreements that are reached by the nations.

Penalization is essential if peace is to be more than a feverish interlude between wars. And, too, the United Nations can prescribe individual responsibility and punishment on the principles applied at Nürnberg by the Union of Soviet Socialist Republics, the United Kingdom, France, and the United States—a formula certain to benefit the world's future.

In this crisis, we represent not only our governments but, in a larger way, we represent the peoples of the world. We must remember that the peoples do not belong to the governments but that the governments belong to the peoples. We must answer their demands; we must answer the world's longing for peace and security.

In that desire the United States shares ardently and hopefully. The search of science for the absolute weapon has reached fruition in this country. But she stands ready to proscribe and destroy this instrument—to lift its use from death to life—if the world will join in a pact to that end.

In our success lies the promise of a new life, freed from the heart-stopping fears that now beset the world. The beginning of victory for the great ideals for which millions have bled and died lies in building a workable plan. Now we approach fulfilment of the aspirations of mankind. At the end of the road lies the fairer, better, surer life we crave and mean to have.

Only by a lasting peace are liberties and democracies strengthened and deepened. War is their enemy. And it will not do to believe that any of us can escape war's devastation. Victor, vanquished, and neutrals alike are affected physically, economically, and morally.

Against the degradation of war we can erect a safeguard. That is the guerdon for which we reach. Within the scope of the formula we outline here there will be found, to those who seek it, the essential elements of our purpose. Others will see only emptiness. Each of us carries his own mirror in which is reflected hope—or determined desperation—courage or cowardice.

There is a famine throughout the world today. It starves men's bodies. But there is a greater famine—the hunger of men's spirit. That starvation can be cured by the conquest of fear, and the substitution of hope, from which springs faith—faith in each other, faith that we want to work together toward salvation, and determination that those who threaten the peace and safety shall be punished.

The peoples of these democracies gathered here have a particular concern with our answer, for their peoples hate war. They will have a heavy exaction to make of those who fail to provide an escape. They are not afraid of an internationalism that protects; they are unwilling to be fobbed off by mouthings about narrow sovereignty, which is today's phrase for yesterday's isolation.

The basis of a sound foreign policy, in this new age, for all the nations here gathered, is that anything that happens, no matter where or how, which menaces the peace of the world, or the economic stability, concerns each and all of us.

That, roughly, may be said to be the central theme of the United Nations. It is with that thought we begin consideration of the most important subject that can engage mankind—life itself.

Let there be no quibbling about the duty and the responsibility of this group and of the governments we represent. I was moved, in the afternoon of my life, to add my effort to gain the world's quest, by the broad mandate under which we were created. The resolution of the General Assembly, passed January 24, 1946 in London, reads:

"Section V. Terms of Reference of the Commission
"The Commission shall proceed with the utmost despatch and enquire into all phases of the problems, and make such recommendations from time to time with respect to them as it finds possible. In particular the Commission shall make specific proposals:

"(*a*) For extending between all nations the exchange of basic scientific information for peaceful ends;

"(*b*) For control of atomic energy to the extent necessary to ensure its use only for peaceful purposes;

"(*c*) For the elimination from national armaments of atomic weapons and of all other major weapons adaptable to mass destruction;

"(*d*) For effective safeguards by way of inspection and other means to protect complying States against the hazards of violations and evasions.

"The work of the Commission should proceed by separate stages, the successful completion of each of which will develop the necessary confidence of the world before the next stage is undertaken. . . ."

Our mandate rests, in text and in spirit, upon the outcome of the Conference in Moscow of Messrs. Molotov of the Union of Soviet Socialist Republics, Bevin of the United Kingdom, and Byrnes of the United States of America. The three Foreign Ministers on December 27, 1945 proposed the establishment of this body.

Their action was animated by a preceding conference in Washington on November 15, 1945, when the President of the United States, associated with Mr. Attlee, Prime Minister of the United Kingdom, and Mr. Mackenzie King, Prime Minister of Canada, stated that international control of the whole field of atomic energy was immediately essential. They proposed the formation of this body. In examining that source, the Agreed Declaration, it will be found that the fathers of the concept recognized the final means of world salvation—the abolition of war. Solemnly they wrote:

"We are aware that the only complete protection for the civilized world from the destructive use of scientific knowledge lies in the prevention of war. No system of safeguards that can be devised will of itself provide an effective guarantee against production of atomic weapons by a nation bent on aggression. Nor can we ignore the possibility of the development of other weapons, or of new methods of warfare, which may constitute as great a threat to civilization as the military use of atomic energy."

Through the historical approach I have outlined, we find ourselves here to test if man can produce, through his will and faith, the miracle of peace, just as he has, through science and skill, the miracle of the atom.

The United States proposes the creation of an International Atomic Development Authority, to which should be entrusted all phases of the development and use of atomic energy, starting with the raw material and including—

1. Managerial control or ownership of all atomic-energy activities potentially dangerous to world security.

2. Power to control, inspect, and license all other atomic activities.

3. The duty of fostering the beneficial uses of atomic energy.

4. Research and development responsibilities of an affirmative character intended to put the Authority in the forefront of atomic knowledge and thus to enable it to comprehend, and therefore to detect, misuse of atomic energy. To be effective, the Authority must itself

be the world's leader in the field of atomic knowledge and development and thus supplement its legal authority with the great power inherent in possession of leadership in knowledge.

I offer this as a basis for beginning our discussion.

But I think the peoples we serve would not believe—and without faith nothing counts—that a treaty, merely outlawing possession or use of the atomic bomb, constitutes effective fulfilment of the instructions to this Commission. Previous failures have been recorded in trying the method of simple renunciation, unsupported by effective guaranties of security and armament limitation. No one would have faith in that approach alone.

Now, if ever, is the time to act for the common good. Public opinion supports a world movement toward security. If I read the signs aright, the peoples want a program not composed merely of pious thoughts but of enforceable sanctions—an international law with teeth in it.

We of this nation, desirous of helping to bring peace to the world and realizing the heavy obligations upon us arising from our possession of the means of producing the bomb and from the fact that it is part of our armament, are prepared to make our full contribution toward effective control of atomic energy.

When an adequate system for control of atomic energy, including the renunciation of the bomb as a weapon, has been agreed upon and put into effective operation and condign punishments set up for violations of the rules of control which are to be stigmatized as international crimes, we propose that—

1. Manufacture of atomic bombs shall stop;

2. Existing bombs shall be disposed of pursuant to the terms of the treaty; and

3. The Authority shall be in possession of full information as to the know-how for the production of atomic energy.

Let me repeat, so as to avoid misunderstanding: My country is ready to make its full contribution toward the end we seek, subject of course to our constitutional processes and to an adequate system of control becoming fully effective, as we finally work it out.

Now as to violations: In the agreement, penalties of as serious a nature as the nations may wish and as immediate and certain in their execution as possible should be fixed for—

1. Illegal possession or use of an atomic bomb;
2. Illegal possession, or separation, of atomic material suitable for use in an atomic bomb;
3. Seizure of any plant or other property belonging to or licensed by the Authority;
4. Wilful interference with the activities of the Authority;
5. Creation or operation of dangerous projects in a manner contrary to, or in the absence of, a license granted by the international control body.

It would be a deception, to which I am unwilling to lend myself, were I not to say to you and to our peoples that the matter of punishment lies at the very heart of our present security system. It might as well be admitted, here and now, that the subject goes straight to the veto power contained in the Charter of the United Nations so far as it relates to the field of atomic energy. The Charter permits penalization only by concurrence of each of the five great powers—the Union of Soviet Socialist Republics, the United Kingdom, China, France, and the United States.

I want to make very plain that I am concerned here with the veto power only as it affects this particular problem. There must be no veto to protect those who violate their solemn agreements not to develop or use atomic energy for destructive purposes.

The bomb does not wait upon debate. To delay may be to die. The time between violation and preventive action or punishment would be all too short for extended discussion as to the course to be followed.

As matters now stand several years may be necessary for another country to produce a bomb, *de novo*. However, once the basic information is generally known, and the Authority has established producing plants for peaceful purposes in the several countries, an illegal seizure of such a plant might permit a malevolent nation to produce a bomb in 12 months, and if preceded by secret preparation and necessary facilities perhaps even in a much shorter time. The time required—the advance warning given of the possible use of a bomb—can only be generally estimated but obviously will depend upon many factors, including the success with which the Authority has been able to introduce elements of safety in the design of its plants and the degree to which illegal and secret preparation for the military use of atomic energy will have been eliminated. Presumably no nation would think of starting a war with only one bomb.

This shows how imperative speed is in detecting and penalizing violations.

The process of prevention and penalization—a problem of profound statecraft—is, as I read it, implicit in the Moscow statement, signed by the Union of Soviet Socialist Republics, the United States, and the United Kingdom a few months ago.

But before a country is ready to relinquish any winning weapons it must have more than words to reassure it. It must have a guarantee of safety, not only against the offenders in the atomic area but against the illegal users of other weapons—bacteriological, biological, gas—perhaps—why not? against war itself.

In the elimination of war lies our solution, for only then will nations cease to compete with one another in the production and use of dread "secret" weapons which are evaluated solely by their capacity to kill. This devilish program takes us back not merely to the Dark Ages but from cosmos to chaos. If we succeed in finding a suitable way to control atomic weapons, it is reasonable to hope that we may also preclude the use of other weapons adaptable to mass destruction. When a man learns to say "A" he can, if he chooses, learn the rest of the alphabet too.

Let this be anchored in our minds:

Peace is never long preserved by weight of metal or by an armament race. Peace can be made tranquil and secure only by understanding and agreement fortified by sanctions. We must embrace international cooperation or international disintegration.

Science has taught us how to put the atom to work. But to make it work for good instead of for evil lies in the domain dealing with the principles of human duty. We are now facing a problem more of ethics than of physics.

The solution will require apparent sacrifice in pride and in position, but better pain as the price of peace than death as the price of war.

I now submit the following measures as representing the fundamental features of a plan which would give effect to certain of the conclusions which I have epitomized.

1. *General.* The Authority should set up a thorough plan for control of the field of atomic energy, through various forms of

ownership, dominion, licenses, operation, inspection, research, and management by competent personnel. After this is provided for, there should be as little interference as may be with the economic plans and the present private, corporate, and state relationships in the several countries involved.

2. *Raw Materials.* The Authority should have as one of its earliest purposes to obtain and maintain complete and accurate information on world supplies of uranium and thorium and to bring them under its dominion. The precise pattern of control for various types of deposits of such materials will have to depend upon the geological, mining, refining, and economic facts involved in different situations.

The Authority should conduct continuous surveys so that it will have the most complete knowledge of the world geology of uranium and thorium. Only after all current information on world sources of uranium and thorium is known to us all can equitable plans be made for their production, refining, and distribution.

3. *Primary Production Plants.* The Authority should exercise complete managerial control of the production of fissionable materials. This means that it should control and operate all plants producing fissionable materials in dangerous quantities and must own and control the product of these plants.

4. *Atomic Explosives.* The Authority should be given sole and exclusive right to conduct research in the field of atomic explosives. Research activities in the field of atomic explosives are essential in order that the Authority may keep in the forefront of knowledge in the field of atomic energy and fulfil the objective of preventing illicit manufacture of bombs. Only by maintaining its position as the best-informed agency will the Authority be able to determine the line between intrinsically dangerous and non-dangerous activities.

5. *Strategic Distribution of Activities and Materials.* The activities entrusted exclusively to the Authority because they are intrinsically dangerous to security should be distributed throughout the world. Similarly, stockpiles of raw materials and fissionable materials should not be centralized.

6. *Non-Dangerous Activities.* A function of the Authority should be promotion of the peaceful benefits of atomic energy.

Atomic research (except in explosives), the use of research reactors, the production of radioactive traces by means of non-dangerous reactors, the use of such tracers, and to some extent the production of power should be open to nations and their citizens under reasonable licensing arrangements from the Authority. Denatured materials, whose use we know also requires suitable safeguards, should be furnished for such purposes by the Authority under lease or other arrangement. Denaturing seems to have been overestimated by the public as a safety measure.

7. *Definition of Dangerous and Non-Dangerous Activities.* Although a reasonable dividing line can be drawn between dangerous and non-dangerous activities, it is not hard and fast. Provision should, therefore, be made to assure constant reexamination of the questions and to permit revision of the dividing line as changing conditions and new discoveries may require.

8. *Operations of Dangerous Activities.* Any plant dealing with uranium or thorium after it once reaches the potential of dangerous use must be not only subject to the most rigorous and competent inspection by the Authority, but its actual operation shall be under the management, supervision, and control of the Authority.

9. *Inspection.* By assigning intrinsically dangerous activities exclusively to the Authority, the difficulties of inspection are reduced. If the Authority is the only agency which may lawfully conduct dangerous activities, then visible operation by others than the Authority will constitute an unambiguous danger signal. Inspection will also occur in connection with the licensing functions of the Authority.

10. *Freedom of Access.* Adequate ingress and egress for all qualified representatives of the Authority must be assured. Many of the inspection activities of the Authority should grow out of, and be incidental to, its other functions. Important measures of inspection will be associated with the tight control of raw materials, for this is a keystone of the plan. The continuing activities of prospecting, survey, and research in relation to raw materials will be designed not only to serve the affirmative development functions of the Authority but also to assure that no surreptitious operations are conducted in the raw-materials field by nations or their citizens.

11. *Personnel.* The personnel of the Authority should be recruited on a basis of proven competence but also so far as possible on an international basis.

12. *Progress by Stages.* A primary step in the creation of the

system of control is the setting forth, in comprehensive terms, of the functions, responsibilities, powers, and limitations of the Authority. Once a charter for the Authority has been adopted, the Authority and the system of control for which it will be responsible will require time to become fully organized and effective. The plan of control will, therefore, have to come into effect in successive stages. These should be specifically fixed in the charter or means should be otherwise set forth in the charter for transitions from one stage to another, as contemplated in the resolution of the United Nations Assembly which created this Commission.

13. *Disclosures.* In the deliberations of the United Nations Commission on Atomic Energy, the United States is prepared to make available the information essential to a reasonable understanding of the proposals which it advocates. Further disclosures must be dependent, in the interests of all, upon the effective ratification of the treaty. When the Authority is actually created, the United States will join the other nations in making available the further information essential to that organization for the performance of its functions. As the successive stages of international control are reached, the United States will be prepared to yield, to the extent required by each stage, national control of activities in this field to the Authority.

14. *International Control.* There will be questions about the extent of control to be allowed to national bodies, when the Authority is established. Purely national authorities for control and development of atomic energy should to the extent necessary for the effective operation of the Authority be subordinate to it. This is neither an endorsement nor a disapproval of the creation of national authorities. The Commission should evolve a clear demarcation of the scope of duties and responsibilities of such national authorities.

And now I end. I have submitted an outline for present discussion. Our consideration will be broadened by the criticism of the United States proposals and by the plans of the other nations, which, it is to be hoped, will be submitted at their early convenience. I and my associates of the United States Delegation will make available to each member of this body books and pamphlets, including the Acheson-Lilienthal report, recently made by the United States Department of State, and the McMahon Committee Monograph No. 1 entitled "Essential Information on Atomic Energy" relating to the McMahon bill recently passed by the United States Senate, which may prove of value in assessing the situation.

All of us are consecrated to making an end of gloom and hopelessness. It will not be an easy job. The way is long and thorny, but supremely worth traveling. All of us want to stand erect, with our faces to the sun, instead of being forced to burrow into the earth, like rats.

The pattern of salvation must be worked out by all for all.

The light at the end of the tunnel is dim, but our path seems to grow brighter as we actually begin our journey. We cannot yet light the way to the end. However, we hope the suggestions of my Government will be illuminating.

Let us keep in mind the exhortation of Abraham Lincoln, whose words, uttered at a moment of shattering national peril, form a complete text for our deliberation. I quote, paraphrasing slightly:

"We cannot escape history. We of this meeting will be remembered in spite of ourselves. No personal significance or insignificance can spare one or another of us. The fiery trial through which we are passing will light us down in honor or dishonor to the latest generation.

"We say we are for Peace. The world will not forget that we say this. We know how to save Peace. The world knows that we do. We, even we here, hold the power and have the responsibility.

"We shall nobly save, or meanly lose, the last, best hope of earth. The way is plain, peaceful, generous, just—a way which, if followed, the world will forever applaud."

My thanks for your attention.

Aerial Inspection Proposals Submitted by the Western Powers and the Soviet Union

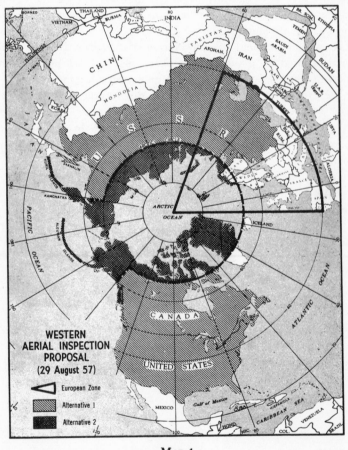

MAP 1

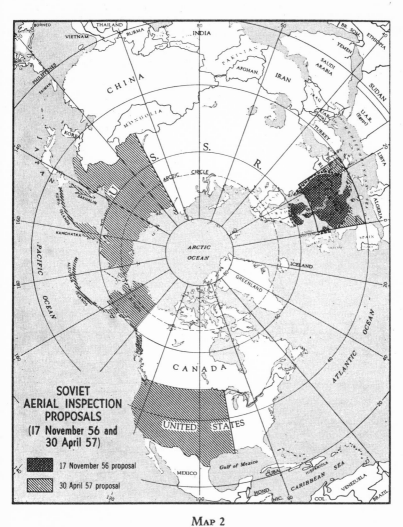

MAP 2

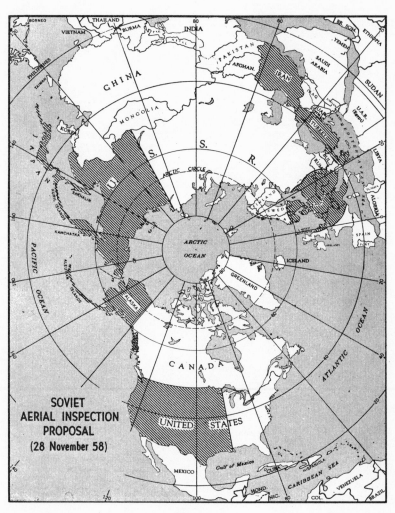

SOVIET
AERIAL INSPECTION
PROPOSAL
(28 November 58)

MAP 3

Treaty Banning Nuclear Weapon Tests in the Atmosphere, in Outer Space, and Under Water

The Governments of the United States of America, the United Kingdom of Great Britain and Northern Ireland, and the Union of Soviet Socialist Republics, hereinafter referred to as the "Original Parties",

Proclaiming as their principal aim the speediest possible achievement of an agreement on general and complete disarmament under strict international control in accordance with the objectives of the United Nations which would put an end to the armaments race and eliminate the incentive to the production and testing of all kinds of weapons, including nuclear weapons,

Seeking to achieve the discontinuance of all test explosions of nuclear weapons for all time, determined to continue negotiations to this end, and desiring to put an end to the contamination of man's environment by radioactive substances,

Have agreed as follows:

Article I

1. Each of the Parties to this Treaty undertakes to prohibit, to prevent, and not to carry out any nuclear weapon test explosion, or

any other nuclear explosion, at any place under its jurisdiction or control:

(a) in the atmosphere; beyond its limits, including outer space; or underwater, including territorial waters or high seas; or

(b) in any other environment if such explosion causes radioactive debris to be present outside the territorial limits of the State under whose jurisdiction or control such explosion is conducted. It is understood in this connection that the provisions of this subparagraph are without prejudice to the conclusion of a treaty resulting in the permanent banning of all nuclear test explosions, including all such explosions underground, the conclusion of which, as the Parties have stated in the Preamble to this Treaty, they seek to achieve.

2. Each of the Parties to this Treaty undertakes furthermore to refrain from causing, encouraging, or in any way participating in, the carrying out of any nuclear weapon test explosion, or any other nuclear explosion, anywhere which would take place in any of the environments described, or have the effect referred to, in paragraph 1 of this Article.

Article II

1. Any Party may propose amendments to this Treaty. The text of any proposed amendment shall be submitted to the Depositary Governments which shall circulate it to all Parties of this Treaty. Thereafter, if requested to do so by one-third or more of the Parties, the Depositary Governments shall convene a conference, to which they shall invite all the Parties, to consider such amendment.

2. Any amendment to this Treaty must be approved by a majority of the votes of all the Parties to this Treaty, including the votes of all of the Original Parties. The amendment shall enter into force for all Parties upon the deposit of instruments of ratification by a majority of all the Parties, including the instruments of ratification of all of the Original Parties.

Article III

1. This Treaty shall be open to all States for signature. Any State which does not sign this Treaty before its entry into force in accordance with paragraph 3 of this Article may accede to it at any time.

2. This Treaty shall be subject to ratification by signatory States. Instruments of ratification and instruments of accession shall be deposited with the Governments of the Original Parties—the United States of America, the United Kingdom of Great Britain and Northern Ireland, and the Union of Soviet Socialist Republics—which are hereby designated the Depositary Governments.

3. This Treaty shall enter into force after its ratification by all the Original Parties and the deposit of their instruments of ratification.

4. For States whose instruments of ratification or accession are deposited subsequent to the entry into force of this Treaty, it shall enter into force on the date of the deposit of their instruments of ratification or accession.

5. The Depositary Governments shall promptly inform all signatory and acceding States of the date of each signature, the date of deposit of each instrument of ratification of and accession to this Treaty, the date of its entry into force, and the date of receipt of any requests for conferences or other notices.

6. This Treaty shall be registered by the Depositary Governments pursuant to Article 102 of the Charter of the United Nations.

Article IV

This Treaty shall be of unlimited duration.

Each Party shall in exercising its national sovereignty have the right to withdraw from the Treaty if it decides that extraordinary events, related to the subject matter of this Treaty, have jeopardized the supreme interests of its country. It shall give notice of such withdrawal to all other Parties to the Treaty three months in advance.

Article V

This Treaty, of which the English and Russian texts are equally authentic, shall de deposited in the archives of the Depositary Governments. Duly certified copies of this Treaty shall be transmitted by the Depositary Governments to the Governments of the signatory and acceding States.

In witness whereof the undersigned, duly authorized, have signed this Treaty.

DONE in triplicate at the city of Moscow the fifth day of August, one thousand nine hundred and sixty-three.

For the Government of the United States of America	For the Government of the United Kingdom of Great Britain and Northern Ireland	For the Government of the Union of Soviet Socialist Republics

Treaty on the Nonproliferation of Nuclear Weapons July 1, 1968

The States concluding this Treaty, hereinafter referred to as the "Parties to the Treaty,"

Considering the devastation that would be visited upon all mankind by a nuclear war and the consequent need to make every effort to avert the danger of such a war and to take measures to safeguard the security of peoples,

Believing that the proliferation of nuclear weapons would seriously enhance the danger of nuclear war,

In conformity with resolutions of the United Nations General Assembly calling for the conclusion of an agreement on the prevention of wider dissemination of nuclear weapons,

Undertaking to cooperate in facilitating the application of International Atomic Energy safeguards on peaceful nuclear activities.

Expressing their support for research, development and other efforts to further the application, within the framework of the International Atomic Energy Agency safeguards system, of the principle of safeguarding effectively the flow of source and special fissionable materials by use of instruments and other techniques at certain strategic points,

Affirming the principle that the benefits of peaceful applications of nuclear technology, including any technological by-products which may be derived by nuclear-weapon States from the development of nuclear explosive devices, should be available for peaceful purposes to all Parties to the Treaty, whether nuclear-weapon or non-nuclear-weapon States,

Convinced that, in furtherance of this principle, all Parties to the Treaty are entitled to participate in the fullest possible exchange of scientific information for, and to contribute alone or in cooperation with other States to, the further development of the applications of atomic energy for peaceful purposes,

Declaring their intention to achieve at the earliest possible date the cessation of the nuclear arms race and to undertake effective measures in the direction of nuclear disarmament,

Urging the cooperation of all States in the attainment of this objective,

Recalling the determination expressed by the Parties to the 1963 Treaty banning nuclear weapon tests in the atmosphere, in outer space and under water in its Preamble to seek to achieve the discontinuance of all test explosions of nuclear weapons for all time and to continue negotiations to this end,

Desiring to further the easing of international tension and the strengthening of trust between States in order to facilitate the cessation of the manufacture of nuclear weapons, the liquidation of all their existing stockpiles, and the elimination from national arsenals of nuclear weapons and the means of their delivery pursuant to a treaty on general and complete disarmament under strict and effective international control,

Recalling that, in accordance with the Charter of the United Nations, States must refrain in their international relations from the threat or use of force against the territorial integrity or political independence of any State, or in any other manner inconsistent with the Purposes of the United Nations, and that the establishment and maintenance of international peace and security are to be promoted with the least diversion for armaments of the world's human and economic resources,

Have agreed as follows:

Article I

Each nuclear-weapon State Party to the Treaty undertakes not to transfer to any recipient whatsoever nuclear weapons or other nuclear explosive devices or control over such weapons or explosive devices directly, or indirectly; and not in any way to assist, encourage, or induce any non-nuclear-weapon State to manufacture or otherwise acquire nuclear weapons or other nuclear explosive devices, or control over such weapons or explosive devices.

Article II

Each non-nuclear-weapon State Party to the Treaty undertakes not to receive the transfer from any transferor whatsoever of nuclear weapons or other nuclear explosive devices or of control over such weapons or explosive devices directly, or indirectly; not to manufacture or otherwise acquire nuclear weapons or other nuclear explosive devices; and not to seek or receive any assistance in the manufacture of nuclear weapons or other nuclear explosive devices.

Article III

1. Each non-nuclear-weapon State Party to the Treaty undertakes to accept safeguards, as set forth in an agreement to be negotiated and concluded with the International Atomic Energy Agency in accordance with the Statute of the International Atomic Energy Agency and the Agency's safeguards system, for the exclusive purpose of verification of the fulfillment of its obligations assumed under this Treaty with a view to preventing diversion of nuclear energy from peaceful uses to nuclear weapons or other nuclear explosive devices. Procedures for the safeguards required by this article shall be followed with respect to source or special fissionable material whether it is being produced, processed or used in any principal nuclear facility or is outside any such facility. The safeguards required by this article shall be applied on all source or special fissionable material in all peaceful nuclear activities within the territory of such State, under its jurisdiction, or carried out under its control anywhere.

2. Each State Party to the Treaty undertakes not to provide: (a) source or special fissionable material, or (b) equipment or material especially designed or prepared for the processing, use or production of special fissionable material, to any non-nuclear-weapon State for peaceful purposes, unless the source or special fissionable material shall be subject to the safeguards required by this article.

3. The safeguards required by this article shall be implemented in a manner designed to comply with article IV of this Treaty, and to avoid hampering the economic or technological development of the Parties or international cooperation in the field of peaceful nuclear activities, including the international exchange of nuclear material and equipment for the processing, use or production of nuclear material for peaceful purposes in accordance with the provisions of this article and the principle of safeguarding set forth in the Preamble of the Treaty.

4. Non-nuclear-weapon States Party to the Treaty shall conclude agreements with the International Atomic Energy Agency to meet the requirements of this article either individually or together with other States in accordance with the Statute of the International Atomic Energy Agency. Negotiation of such agreements shall commence within 180 days from the original entry into force of this Treaty. For States depositing their instruments of ratification or accession after the 180-day period, negotiation of such agreements shall commence not later than the date of such deposit. Such agreements shall enter into force not later than eighteen months after the date of initiation of negotiations.

Article IV

1. Nothing in this Treaty shall be interpreted as affecting the inalienable right of all the Parties to the Treaty to develop research, production and use of nuclear energy for peaceful purposes without discrimination and in conformity with articles I and II of this Treaty.

2. All the Parties to the Treaty undertake to facilitate, and have the right to participate in, the fullest possible exchange of equipment, materials, and scientific and technological information for the peaceful uses of nuclear energy. Parties to the Treaty in a position to do so shall also cooperate in contributing alone or together with other States or international organizations to the further development of the applications of nuclear energy for peaceful purposes, especially in the territories of non-nuclear-weapon States Party to the Treaty, with due consideration for the needs of the developing areas of the world.

Article V

Each Party to the Treaty undertakes to take appropriate measures to ensure that, in accordance with this Treaty, under appropriate international observation and through appropriate international procedures, potential benefits from any peaceful applications of nuclear explosions will be made available to non-nuclear-weapon States Party to the Treaty on a non-discriminatory basis and that the charge to such Parties for the explosive devices used will be as low as possible and exclude any charge for research and development. Non-nuclear-weapon States Party to the Treaty shall be able to obtain such benefits, pursuant to a special international agreement or agreements, through an appropriate international body with adequate representation of non-nuclear-weapon States. Negotiations on this subject shall commence as soon as possible after the Treaty enters into force. Non-nuclear-weapon States Party to the Treaty so desiring may also obtain such benefits pursuant to bilaterial agreements.

Article VI

Each of the Parties to the Treaty undertakes to pursue negotiations in good faith on effective measures relating to cessation of the nuclear arms race at an early date and to nuclear disarmament, and on a treaty on general and complete disarmament under strict and effective international control.

Article VII

Nothing in this Treaty affects the right of any group of States to conclude regional treaties in order to assure the total absence of nuclear weapons in their respective territories.

Article VIII

1. Any Party to the Treaty may propose amendments to this Treaty. The text of any proposed amendment shall be submitted to the Depositary Governments which shall circulate it to all Parties to the Treaty. Thereupon, if requested to do so by one-third or more of the Parties to the Treaty, the Depositary Governments shall convene

a conference, to which they shall invite all the Parties to the Treaty, to consider such an amendment.

2. Any amendment to this Treaty must be approved by a majority of the votes of all the Parties to the Treaty, including the votes of all nuclear-weapon States Party to the Treaty and all other Parties which, on the date the amendment is circulated, are members of the Board of Governors of the International Atomic Energy Agency. The amendment shall enter into force for each Party that deposits its instrument of ratification of the amendment upon the deposit of such instruments of ratification by a majority of all the Parties, including the instruments of ratification of all nuclear-weapon States Party to the Treaty and all other Parties which, on the date the amendment is circulated, are members of the Board of Governors of the International Atomic Energy Agency. Thereafter, it shall enter into force for any other Party upon the deposit of its instrument of ratification of the amendment.

3. Five years after the entry into force of this Treaty, a conference of Parties to the Treaty shall be held in Geneva, Switzerland, in order to review the operation of this Treaty with a view to assuring that the purposes of the Preamble and the provisions of the Treaty are being realized. At intervals of five years thereafter, a majority of the Parties to the Treaty may obtain, by submitting a proposal to this effect to the Depositary Governments, the convening of further conferences with the same objective of reviewing the operation of the Treaty.

Article IX

1. This Treaty shall be open to all States for signature. Any State which does not sign the Treaty before its entry into force in accordance with paragraph 3 of this article may accede to it at any time.

2. This Treaty shall be subject to ratification by signatory States. Instruments of ratification and instruments of accession shall be deposited with the Governments of the United States of America, the United Kingdom of Great Britain and Northern Ireland and the Union of Soviet Socialist Republics, which are hereby designated the Depository Governments.

3. This Treaty shall enter into force after its ratification by the States, the Governments of which are designated Depositaries of the

Treaty, and forty other States signatory to this Treaty and the deposits of their instruments of ratification. For the purposes of this Treaty, a nuclear-weapon State is one which has manufactured and exploded a nuclear weapon or other nuclear explosive device prior to January 1, 1967.

4. For States whose instruments of ratification or accession are deposited subsequent to the entry into force of this Treaty, it shall enter into force on the date of the deposit of their instruments of ratification or accession.

5. The Depositary Governments shall promptly inform all signatory and acceding States of the date of each signature, the date of deposit of each instrument of ratification or of accession, the date of the entry into force of this Treaty, and the date of receipt of any requests for convening a conference or other notices.

6. This Treaty shall be registered by the Depositary Governments pursuant to article 102 of the Charter of the United Nations.

Article X

1. Each Party shall in exercising its national sovereignty have the right to withdraw from the Treaty if it decides that extraordinary events, related to the subject matter of this Treaty, have jeopardized the supreme interests of its country. It shall give notice of such withdrawal to all other Parties to the Treaty and to the United Nations Security Council three months in advance. Such notice shall include a statement of the extraordinary events it regards as having jeopardized its supreme interests.

2. Twenty-five years after the entry into force of the Treaty, a conference shall be convened to decide whether the Treaty shall continue in force indefinitely, or shall be extended for an additional fixed period or periods. This decision shall be taken by a majority of the Parties to the Treaty.

Article XI

This Treaty, the English, Russian, French, Spanish and Chinese texts of which are equally authentic, shall be deposited in the archives of the Depositary Governments. Duly certified copies of this Treaty shall be transmitted by the Depositary Governments to the Governments of the signatory and acceding States.

IN WITNESS WHEREOF the undersigned, duly authorized, have signed this Treaty.

Done in triplicate, at the cities of Washington, London and Moscow, this first day of July one thousand nine hundred sixty-eight.

United Nations Security Council Resolution 255, Adopted by the Security Council at Its 1433d Meeting on 19 June 1968

The Security Council,

Noting with appreciation the desire of a large number of States to subscribe to the Treaty on the Non-Proliferation of Nuclear Weapons, and thereby to undertake not to receive the transfer from any transferor whatsoever of nuclear weapons or other nuclear explosive devices or of control over such weapons or explosive devices directly, or indirectly; not to manufacture or otherwise acquire nuclear weapons or other nuclear explosive devices; and not to seek or receive any assistance in the manufacture of nuclear weapons or other nuclear explosive devices,

Taking into consideration the concern of certain of these States that, in conjunction with their adherence to the Treaty on the Non-Proliferation of Nuclear Weapons, appropriate measures be undertaken to safeguard their security,

Bearing in mind that any aggression accompanied by the use of nuclear weapons would endanger the peace and security of all States,

1. Recognizes that aggression with nuclear weapons or the threat of such aggression against a non-nuclear-weapon State would create a situation in which the Security Council, and above all its nuclear-weapon State, permanent members, would have to act immediately in accordance with their obligations under the United Nations Charter;

2. Welcomes the intention expressed by certain States that they will provide or support immediate assistance, in accordance with the Charter, to any non-nuclear-weapon State Party to the Treaty on the Non-Proliferation of Nuclear Weapons that is a victim of an act or an object of a threat of aggression in which nuclear weapons are used;

3. Reaffirms in particular the inherent right, recognized under Article 51 of the Charter, of individual and collective self-defense if an armed attack occurs against a Member of the United Nations, until the Security Council has taken measures necessary to maintain international peace and security.

Declaration of the Government of the United States of America Made in the United Nations Security Council in Explanation of Its Vote for Security Council Resolution 255

The Government of the United States notes with appreciation the desire expressed by a large number of States to subscribe to the treaty on the non-proliferation of nuclear weapons.

We welcome the willingness of these States to undertake not to receive the transfer from any transferor whatsoever of nuclear weapons or other nuclear explosive devices or of control over such weapons or explosive devices directly, or indirectly; not to manufacture or otherwise acquire nuclear weapons or other nuclear explosive devices; and not to seek or receive any assistance in the manufacture of nuclear weapons or other nuclear explosive devices.

The United States also notes the concern of certain of these States that, in conjunction with their adherence to the treaty on the non-proliferation of nuclear weapons, appropriate measures be undertaken to safeguard their security. Any aggression accompanied by the use of nuclear weapons would endanger the peace and security of all States.

Bearing these considerations in mind, the United States declares the following:

Aggression with nuclear weapons, or the threat of such aggression, against a non-nuclear-weapon State would create a qualitatively new situation in which the nuclear-weapon States which are permanent members of the United Nations Security Council would have to act immediately through the Security Council to take the measures necessary to counter such aggression or to remove the threat of aggression in accordance with the United Nations Charter, which calls for taking "* * * effective collective measures for the prevention and removal of threats to the peace, and for the suppression of acts of aggression or other breaches of the peace * * *". Therefore, any State which commits aggression accompanied by the use of nuclear weapons or which threatens such aggression must be aware that its actions are to be countered effectively by measures to be taken in accordance with the United Nations Charter to suppress the aggression or remove the threat of aggression.

The United States affirms its intention, as a permanent member of the United Nations Security Council, to seek immediate Council action to provide assistance, in accordance with the Charter, to any non-nuclear-weapon State party to the treaty on the non-proliferation of nuclear weapons that is a victim of an act of aggression or an object of a threat of aggression in which nuclear weapons are used.

The United States reaffirms in particular the inherent right, recognized under Article 51 of the Charter, of individual and collective self-defense if an armed attack, including a nuclear attack, occurs against a Member of the United Nations, until the Security Council has taken measures necessary to maintain international peace and security.

The United States vote for the resolution before us and this statement of the way in which the United States intends to act in accordance with the Charter of the United Nations are based upon the fact that the resolution is supported by other permanent members of the Security Council which are nuclear-weapon States and are also proposing to sign the treaty on the non-proliferation of nuclear weapons, and that these States have made similar statements as to the way in which they intend to act in accordance with the Charter.

Bibliography

Books and articles on various aspects of the nuclear years, relatively scarce in the early period, have multiplied in geometric proportions in the past decade. There is now a wealth of detailed material available —most written by Americans, a considerable amount by other non-Communist authors, but still very little by Soviet writers.

Two continuing sources contain essential information: the annual reports of the U.S. Arms Control and Disarmament Agency and the agency's series entitled Documents on Disarmament. The former covers the work of the agency since its founding; the latter contains basic material about arms control efforts since 1945. Both are available from the Government Printing Office, Washington, D.C. Additional primary sources are the publications of the Institute for Strategic Studies, a private, London-based organization. They include the annual Military Balance and Strategic Survey and the Adelphi Papers, reprints of important articles from Eastern and Western sources on issues in the arms field. A most useful Adelphi Paper is No. 63, "Advanced Strategic Missiles: A Short Guide," by Ian Smart (December, 1969). Also important are the annual defense posture statements that were prepared during the years when Robert S. McNamara was U.S. Secretary of Defense. They are invaluable sources of facts and figures about weapons systems and of the diplomatic context surrounding weapons development.

ACHESON, DEAN. *Present at the Creation.* New York: W. W. Norton, 1969. The former Secretary of State's detailed memoirs.

BADER, WILLIAM B. *The United States and the Spread of Nuclear Weapons.* New York: Pegasus, 1968.

BARUCH, BERNARD M. *My Own Story.* New York: Holt, Rinehart and Winston, 1957.

BEAL, JOHN ROBINSON. *John Foster Dulles: 1888–1959.* New York: Harper & Bros., 1959. A highly favorable account of a powerful Secretary of State.

BECHHOEFER, BERNHARD G. *Postwar Negotiations for Arms Control.* Washington, D.C.: The Brookings Institution, 1961. The definitive account of what occurred from the genesis of the Baruch Plan through 1960.

BYRNES, JAMES F. *Speaking Frankly.* New York: Harper & Bros., 1947. Includes the former Secretary of State's version of his differences with President Truman.

CHASE, HAROLD W., and LERMAN, ALLEN H., eds. *Kennedy and the Press.* New York: Thomas Y. Crowell, 1965. An annotated collection of the President's press conferences.

CHAYES, ABRAM, and WIESNER, JEROME B., eds. *ABM.* New York: Harper & Row, 1969. A melange of authors explain why they believe the ABM is not needed.

CLEMENS, WALTER C., JR., *The Arms Race and Sino-Soviet Relations.* Stanford, Calif.: The Hoover Institution, 1968. A well-documented, conservative view.

DALLIN, ALEXANDER, et al. *The Soviet Union and Disarmament.* New York: Praeger, 1964. A discussion of Soviet rationale and behavior to which Larson, cited below, is the sequel.

DJILAS, MILOVAN. *Conversations with Stalin.* New York: Harcourt, Brace & World, 1962. A rare glimpse into Stalin's postwar thinking.

EISENHOWER, DWIGHT D. *White House Years.* 2 vols. Garden City, N.Y.: Doubleday, 1963–65.

FLEMING, DENNA F. *The Cold War and Its Origins, 1917–60.* 2 vols. Garden City, N.Y.: Doubleday, 1961. An early version of revisionist history in which most of the blame is attached to the United States.

FONTAINE, ANDRÉ. *History of the Cold War.* 2 vols. New York: Pantheon, 1968–69. The account of an eminent French journalist from a perspective outside the capitals of the two major antagonists.

GARTHOFF, RAYMOND L. *Soviet Military Policy.* New York: Praeger, 1966. One of many useful works by a leading analyst who is also a practitioner for the U.S. Government.

GRODZINS, MORTON, and RABINOWITCH, EUGENE, eds. *The Atomic Age.* New York: Basic Books, 1963. A collection of articles from the *Bulletin of Atomic Scientists*, 1945 to 1962.

HALLE, LOUIS J. *The Cold War as History.* New York: Harper & Row, 1967. A lucid explanation in which the Marshall Plan's role is emphasized.

HILSMAN, ROGER. *To Move a Nation.* Garden City, N.Y.: Doubleday, 1967. A spirited and partisan view of the politics of foreign policy in the Kennedy era.

HORELICK, ARNOLD L., and RUSH, MYRON. *Strategic Power and Soviet Foreign Policy.* Chicago: University of Chicago Press, 1966. A well-documented RAND study.

KISSINGER, HENRY A. *Nuclear Weapons and Foreign Policy.* New York: Harper & Bros., 1957.

LAMONT, LANSING. *Day of Trinity.* New York: Atheneum, 1965. How it all began at Alamogordo, in fascinating detail.

LARSON, THOMAS B. *Disarmament and Soviet Policy, 1964–68.* Englewood Cliffs, N.J.: Prentice-Hall, 1960. Highly useful sequel to Dallin, cited above.

LILIENTHAL, DAVID E. *The Atomic Energy Years, 1945–50.* Vol. 2 of The Journals of David E. Lilienthal. New York: Harper & Row, 1964. Contemporary memoranda on the Truman era.

MACMILLAN, HAROLD. *Tides of Fortune, 1945–55.* New York: Harper & Row, 1969. A less-than-satisfactory British account of a turbulent decade.

SCHLESINGER, ARTHUR M., JR. *A Thousand Days: John F. Kennedy in the White House.* Boston: Houghton Mifflin, 1965.

SCHUBERT, JACK, and LAPP, RALPH E. *Radiation: What It Is and How It Affects You.* New York: The Viking Press, 1957.

SIDEY, HUGH. *John F. Kennedy, President.* New York: Atheneum, 1963. Best of the journalists' histories of the Kennedy era.

SNOW, EDGAR. *The Other Side of the River.* New York: Random House, 1961. Contemporary China as seen by one of those rare people with access to Mao Tse-tung.

SOKOLOVSKII, V., ed. *Soviet Military Strategy.* Englewood Cliffs, N.J.: Prentice-Hall, 1963. A RAND translation of an important Soviet work. Annotated.

SORENSEN, THEODORE H. *Kennedy.* New York: Harper & Row, 1965.

STERN, PHILIP M. (with the collaboration of HAROLD P. GREEN). *The Oppenheimer Case: Security on Trial.* New York: Harper & Row, 1969. An absorbing and definitive account of a celebrated case.

TATU, MICHEL. *Power in the Kremlin: From Khrushchev to Kosygin.* New York: The Viking Press, 1969. A detailed examination by a long-time Moscow correspondent of *Le Monde.*

TRUMAN, HARRY S. *Memoirs.* 2 vols. Garden City, N.Y.: Doubleday, 1955–56.

ULAM, ADAM B. *Expansion and Coexistence: The History of Soviet Foreign Policy, 1917–67.* New York: Praeger, 1968. Probably the best in its field.

VANDENBERG, ARTHUR H., JR., ed. *The Private Papers of Senator Vandenberg.* Boston: Houghton Mifflin, 1952.

WISE, DAVID, and ROSS, THOMAS B. *The Invisible Government.* New York: Random House, 1964. The CIA stripped naked, as nearly as any outsider can do it.

WOLFE, THOMAS W. *Soviet Power and Europe.* 2 vols. Santa Monica, Calif.: The RAND Corporation, 1968–69. Sweeping views and excellent insight. Well documented.

Index